Now You've Been Shortlisted

Your step-by-step guide to being successful at interviews and assessment centres

By Denise Taylor

HARRIMAN HOUSE LTD

3A Penns Road
Petersfield
Hampshire
GU32 2EW
GREAT BRITAIN

Tel: +44 (0)1730 233870
Fax: +44 (0)1730 233880
Email: enquiries@harriman-house
Website: www.harriman-house.co

First published in Great Britain in 2010
Reprinted 2011

Copyright © Harriman House Ltd

The right of Denise Taylor to be identified as author has been asserted in accordance with the Copyright, Design and Patents Acts 1988.

ISBN 13: 978-1906659-32-5

British Library Cataloguing in Publication Data
A CIP catalogue record for this book can be obtained from the British Library.

Exercises on pages 43-44, 59-61 and 74 are copyright © Team Focus 2009. These practice items are reproduced by perrmission from Team Focus Ltd, Heritage House, 13 Bridge Street, Maidenhead, Berkshire SL6 8LR.

Printed and bound by CPI Group (UK) Ltd, Croydon, CR0 4YY

With love and thanks to my long-suffering husband and family who didn't get to see much of me for a few months whilst I was engrossed in writing.

This book is also dedicated to the hundreds of clients I have worked with over the years. Working with you has been an absolute delight, and I'm always so pleased when you get the success you deserve with your job applications.

Contents page

About the Author   vii
Acknowledgements   ix
Preface   xi
Introduction   xiii

Preparation   **1**

Chapter 1. The employer perspective   3
Chapter 2. Preparing for success   9

Psychometric Testing   **21**

Chapter 3. Introducing psychometric tests   23
Chapter 4. Verbal reasoning and critical-thinking tests   39
Chapter 5. Numerical tests   55
Chapter 6. Abstract reasoning and other tests   71
Chapter 7. Personality questionnaires   79

Assessment Centres   **97**

Chapter 8. Assessment centres – an introduction   99
Chapter 9. Group exercises   113
Chapter 10. Written exercises   129
Chapter 11. In-tray exercises   137
Chapter 12. Presentations   143
Chapter 13. Role-plays   153
Chapter 14. Other exercises   165

Interviews 171

Chapter 15. The interview – preparation 173
Chapter 16. Getting ready to answer questions 185
Chapter 17. Over to you – questions to ask at the end
of the interview 203

On the Day and Following Up 211

Chapter 18. Appearance and body language 213
Chapter 19. On the day 219
Chapter 20. Afterwards 231

Success 239

Chapter 21. You've got the job! 241

A Final Word 249

Answers to Psychometric Tests 251

About the Author

Denise Taylor is an award-winning career coach, chartered psychologist and registered guidance practitioner who has been helping people find out who they are, what they want to do and to be successful in their job search for more than 20 years. She is the founder of Amazing People (www.amazingpeople.co.uk) and noted as one of the top career coaches in the UK, working with clients from all over the UK, Europe and beyond.

With a combination of educational credentials and key industry expertise, Denise has specialised in career development for over 20 years, and has published extensively in this area. She has diplomas in coaching and counselling as well as Masters degrees in occupational psychology from Birkbeck College (University of London) and an MBA from the Open University.

Following a career which saw her rise from Post Office counter clerk to assistant director in less than 14 years, Denise moved into running her own career coaching company in 1999.

She works with individuals, students, graduates and career changers – as well as public and private sector recruiters. She trains interviewers as well as interviewees, so the advice of her books is especially effective for those on the receiving end of recruiters' tests and assessment.

Denise was the featured careers coach on ITV's *Tonight* programme 'How Safe is your Job?' (November 2008) and is regularly asked on radio shows to discuss career-related issues. Her articles and comments have featured in a variety of magazines including *SHE*, *Top Santé*, *Woman* and *Home*, *Woman*, Newspapers such as *The Times* and *The Independent* and online at *JobSite*, *Graduate Prospects* and *PR moment*.

Denise has spoken at a number of professional events and conferences including The Open University Business School, Adult Skills and the Institute of Career Guidance.

Denise is the winner of two National Career Awards. In November 2007 she won a National Career Award (sponsored by the *Independent* newspaper) for her Gold Career Programme. In November 2009 she won a second award – for her Job Search Support Programme.

Acknowledgements

With thanks to the testing companies who generously granted their permission to use their psychometric test questions in this book. In alphabetical order:

Criterion Partnership

Pearson Assessments

Perception Business Psychologists

Sadler Consulting

SHL Group

Team Focus

Preface

This book is for you if you want to significantly increase your chance of getting a great job.

Creating a compelling CV and covering letter is not enough. That's just the first step – it gets you to the interview or assessment centre. You then need to perform well in all stages of the assessment process.

Now You've Been Shortlisted is valuable for job seekers at all stages of their career, from undergraduates seeking their first job to mature job seekers looking for a change or to move on up – all who want specific guidance for a forthcoming interview or assessment centre. It is also a great resource for those advising job seekers, including career coaches and university career advisors.

The book is written in a simple and easy-to-understand style, but don't think the content is simplistic. I draw on my 20+ years of assessment centre design and assessor experience to help you understand what assessors are looking for and to increase your chance of success once you are shortlisted.

The book is structured so you can quickly go to the relevant section. The scene is set in the introduction with details of the employer perspective and preparing for success. The next section covers psychometric testing, and following on from the introductory chapter here you will learn how to do your best in verbal reasoning and critical thinking tests in Chapter 4, numerical tests in Chapter 5, abstract reasoning and other tests in Chapter 6, and personality questionnaires in Chapter 7.

How to perform well in assessment centres is covered in the next seven chapters after this. Following an introduction in Chapter 8, there are chapters on group exercises in Chapter 9, written exercises in Chapter 10, in-tray exercises in Chapter 11, presentations in Chapter 12, role-plays in Chapter 13, and other exercises in Chapter 14.

The art of doing well at interview is then covered in three chapters, looking at preparation, answering questions and what to ask at the end of an interview. Chapters then follow on appearance and body language, on the day of the assessment centre/interview, and after the interview, helping you to not only do an in-depth review but guiding you to follow up after the interview to reinforce why you are right for the job.

You are going to increase your chance of success with this book, so the final chapter provides hints and tips on how to create a great impression and be effective in your new job.

This book contains a number of active links but links can change. If you spot any broken links please email: Denise@amazingpeople.co.uk and see the most up to date list at: www.amazingpeople.co.uk/shortlisted.html

Introduction

This book is for anyone who has received a 'you've been shortlisted' letter and wants to feel more confident and prepared for their forthcoming interview or tests at a full assessment centre.

You've got the letter and you've been shortlisted. For some people there will be one interview before they find out if they are successful, but for most it is the start of a series of steps. You could undertake three interviews: an initial interview with a recruitment consultant, an interview with HR and your possible line manager, before a final interview with several people at once. For others it will be an assessment centre with external consultants followed by a final interview with people within the company; or if you are applying to a new and growing company you may get the job offer following a quite informal meeting.

You should keep this book handy, and be ready to refer to it at different stages over the coming weeks. Some of the advice is general and will be relevant to all types of selection events, but others will be specific to a particular stage in the recruitment process. You may feel that you are an old hand at interviews, that you know what to expect, but companies differ in what they say and how they will structure their assessment centre.

Read each piece of communication you get from the company carefully and make sure that you are ready; you don't want to miss out through being over-confident or forgetting to do some vital preparation.

Some people are too nervous and fail to do well through stress and worry. The chapter on the employer perspective should help you to see recruitment from the other side of the desk. I've also included some suggestions for how to harness your nerves to help you.

I was asked to write this book as I have been shortlisting and selecting people for jobs for over 20 years. As a chartered psychologist this is one of my specialist areas, and prior to starting Amazing People I was head of assessor training for the Post Office. This role included designing well over 100 separate assessment centres and assessing at over 1000 assessment centres, including recruiting graduates, distribution specialists, quality managers, and a wide range of other posts including at director level. I have also worked as a consultant to a broad range of industries everything from telecommunications, pharmaceuticals, charities and energy companies to government departments. Companies differ in their style of recruitment and their level of sophistication, so I will cover a range of examples.

Recruiting people for jobs ranging from graduate entrants to senior executives is an expensive process and companies want to make sure that they have made the right decision. Years ago people used to say 'No one ever got sacked for choosing IBM'. This was back in the days when this was the safe option for choosing a computer. There's an element of this with those making the selection decisions. They want to ensure the successful applicant can do the job and has relevant experience, and in many cases would rather choose someone who has done the job over someone with the abilities and skills to learn quickly but who doesn't have a track record. So you may need to work hard to be convincing.

One way to convince your interviewer(s) is to demonstrate that you understand some of the problems and challenges being faced by the company, and that's why research is so important. Chapter 2 talks you through what to find out and how to use this to your advantage at interview.

Decisions on who gets the job are sometimes made on the interview alone, but more and more companies are adding on something extra. This could be a full assessment centre or just some of the assessment centre elements. For example, you might be asked to undertake online psychometric tests in advance of the interview and the interview could also include a presentation. This is not a 'proper' assessment centre but will provide the company with more information on which to base their decision.

We'll be looking at interviews in some depth, covering both general preparation and the specifics to help you with the different types – from an initial telephone interview to a large panel interview. All case studies are based on actual examples used by myself and fellow professionals over the recent past.

Alongside interviews we consider the different sorts of psychometric tests you might face and also the range of activities covered in assessment centres – from group exercises to presentations and role-play exercises. You will read about practical examples of what to do, and more importantly what not to do, to make you stand out from the rest and get the job.

If you are out of work you might be tempted to say yes to any job offer, but will a job be right for you? Accept a job that isn't right and you'll be unhappy and wanting to leave, something that's likely to prove difficult. Your energy will need to be spent on getting to grips with the job you have recently started, and the companies you subsequently apply to may question your commitment if you are willing to leave a job so soon. So in the last section we look at final preparation for starting your new job, how to make a great first impression and what to do and not do.

Wishing you every success in getting a great job!

Denise Taylor
www.amazingpeople.co.uk

Preparation

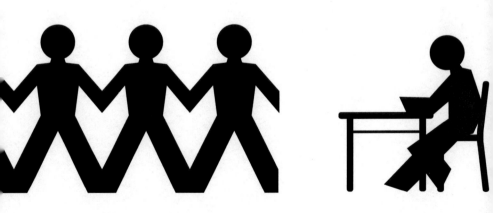

Chapter 1. The employer perspective

Whilst the main focus of this book is on you getting the job offer, let's put this into context. A job is advertised because a company has identified a need for more staff. Sometimes this is a regular occurrence, e.g. the annual graduate recruitment intake, but sometimes it is to fill a specific vacancy. For larger companies there is a clearly defined process, for others it might be less formal, but companies will generally follow these steps:

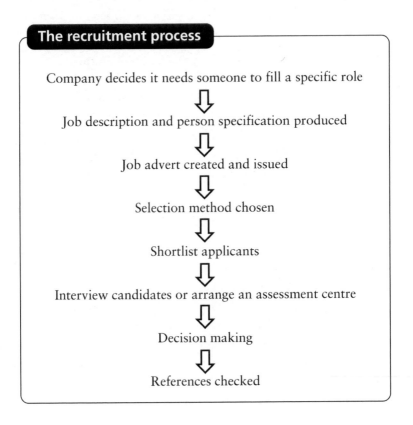

The recruitment process

Company decides it needs someone to fill a specific role

⇩

Job description and person specification produced

⇩

Job advert created and issued

⇩

Selection method chosen

⇩

Shortlist applicants

⇩

Interview candidates or arrange an assessment centre

⇩

Decision making

⇩

References checked

Company decides it needs someone to fill a specific role

This may occur because the company has a vacancy, somebody has left or been promoted, or because there is so much work that they need more staff. There may be a need to convince Human Resources (HR) of the business need and other options might be considered, such as a secondment from another part of the company, or using an interim manager or a temp.

It takes a lot of time and effort to recruit somebody, from the cost of the advert and of external consultants through to training, salary and all associated employment costs, so companies want to get it right. However, it can also be seen as just too much hassle, especially if a company isn't sure of their long-term plans. Will the need still exist in a few months? What if a large order falls through or a supplier goes bust? Sometimes it is easier to make do with temporary staff.

Time needs to be set aside to complete the recruitment process, and it does take time to do it properly. I've spoken with numerous people who are working two jobs because no one has thought to get started on the following steps till at least a month after someone has left, and even then it doesn't become a high priority. This usually results in the overworked employee feeling stressed, taken advantage of and looking for a new job themselves.

Job description and person specification produced

A company should be very clear on what the job involves. A detailed job analysis enables a company to understand the essential elements of the job and what they would consider a successful fulfillment of it. From this can be created a detailed job description (what the job involves). This is then used to create a person specification which outlines the essential and desirable characteristics of the ideal applicant. Together, these documents should help the company get applicants from people with the right skills and abilities and help you as a candidate put a effective application together.

Job advert created and issued

The job advert is designed to attract interest and encourage applicants. It should include any essential requirements so that those who are unsuitable don't apply, but it can't cover all the detail of the job, so this is usually available via the website or on request. It can be particularly helpful for both employer and applicant when a list of essential and desirable criteria are used, as it means applicants can present their most appropriate examples and companies can use this to shortlist. A job advert is also a means of advertising and promoting the company brand, so it will also aim to create a good impression to casual readers.

> I once went on holiday and my boss, thinking he was being helpful as we were very busy, put an ad in the paper for associates to work with me. The ad was so vague I came back to over 600 CVs and covering letters. I had to then compare their applications to criteria they were unaware of, which meant I might have missed some good people and it took up far more time than it should have done.

Selection method chosen

Depending on the level of the job and the type of organisation, a company will decide how to select who gets the job. This could be a series of three interviews – screening interview, main interview and final interview – or it could be a phone interview followed by an assessment centre, or a decision might be made on just one interview.

Ideally, a company will have decided the selection method and date(s) early on so they can let the candidates know the time frame. It can be difficult for people if they only find out they need a whole day for an assessment centre a week beforehand. Companies really should plan in advance as it means they can get interviewers or assessors booked and accommodation organised. If everything is done at the last minute and dates are changed then it doesn't create a good impression.

Shortlist applicants

Shortlisting can be undertaken in-house but is sometimes outsourced to recruitment consultants. Whoever does the shortlisting will be checking the fit between the application and the requirements of the job.

The number of people shortlisted will vary considerably. Some companies will decide to interview perhaps four people for one job, whereas other companies may have so many good people apply that it is difficult to make a decision, and they may opt for a preliminary stage before an assessment centre. This could be done through first interviews, often with a recruitment consultant, through phone interviews or by sending out a list of questions to be answered by email (Chapter 16 includes advice on competency-based questions and is very useful preparation for this).

Interview candidates or arrange an assessment centre

There may be one or several interviews in the selection phase, or the selection may be done through candidates attending an assessment centre. As a candidate you should read the information provided carefully so you know what to expect. The company should compose interview questions to meet the requirements of the job, and design and select relevant assessment centre exercises.

Candidates may be asked to do preparation in advance; they might need to go online for psychometric tests or prepare a presentation. These tasks are covered in subsequent chapters.

Decision making

Decisions will have been taken throughout the process. There is a discussion between HR, the interviewers/assessors and the line manager. The company will take an objective view both on how well they think the candidate can do the job and will also consider organisational fit, i.e. will the applicant fit in? The successful candidate receives a letter or phone call offering them the job and the other candidates are sent the 'regret letter' (we regret to inform you...). Sometimes a candidate may not hear for some time, and this may be because they are in the 'runner up' position just in case the first choice candidate says no.

References and qualifications checked

For some companies this is a formality, but for others it is an essential part of final decision making. You may need to provide evidence of your qualifications and your previous job history may be verified. References will be requested, and for some jobs detailed checks need to be undertaken. If a company subsequently discovers that any details are incorrect they are able to dismiss a candidate, so it is not in anyone's interest to lie.

Chapter 2. Preparing for success

It's brilliant news to get the letter, email or phone call telling you that you've been shortlisted. It means your hard work in applying for the job has been successful, and your CV, covering letter or application form have done their job: in short your preparations have paid off!

Most people will say they prepare for an interview, but usually this just means concentrating on how to answer interview questions. Of course this is important, and is covered in a later chapter, but there is other preparation to do, too, if you want to genuinely stand out.

- Get as much detail as you can from the company

- Review why you applied for the job

- Review why you are going to be perfect for the job

- Find out as much as you can about the company

- Do your research on the industry

- Research so you can ask intelligent questions

- Think about what might be valued at the assessment centre

- Research to give you a psychological advantage

- Notify the company if you have any special needs

- Review any feedback you have received from previous assessment centres

- Review your listening skills

These will all help you be distinctive from the other candidates and increase your chance of success.

Get as much detail as you can from the company

Let's start by looking at what the company will send you. When you receive the correspondence asking you to attend an interview it may tell you:

- The nature of the interview

- Whether there will be any psychometric tests

- Whether it is an assessment centre with group discussion, a presentation, etc.

- Who will interview you (by name and position)

- If you will be given a tour of the company

- Who you will meet

If you don't get this information, request it.

Larger organisations will often send or email an information pack with an invitation to an assessment centre or interview. This should contain the annual report, job description, company details and a map. It may also contain the conditions of employment. Be proactive and ask for anything that isn't included. The job description is important to allow you to prepare for the questions you will be asked – so make sure you receive it. The other information is just as important as it helps you understand more about the company and (especially but not only if you are applying for senior positions) you can demonstrate your strategic thinking by asking business-related questions and also incorporating this knowledge into your answers.

When you get this information, also confirm the interview place, time, day and date:

- In case of a mistake

- As a courtesy

- As another opportunity to record a good impression

Review why you applied for the job

There may be many reasons why you applied for the job, but you might have applied for a number of jobs without really thinking through whether each one was really right for you. So take some time to make sure you do want this job and that it will utilise the skills you want to continue to use.

Often, people are put forward for jobs through working with a recruitment consultant. This can be a great way to find out more about jobs, but the downside is that the consultant will often review your CV, see what you have previously done and put you forward for similar sorts of jobs. This is fine if that's what you want, but if you are trying to reinvent yourself or to move away from your previous roles then you need to decide if this interview will be a good move for you. You are going to need to put in a lot of work to get yourself ready for interview so will this be time well spent?

You may have sent your CV to many different companies without thinking through whether you actually want the job. Do you really want an 80-mile journey to work and back each day? Does working in an engineering or retail company really appeal? You might have been a training manager in the past, and could certainly do it again, but if you really want to move into a role as an internal coach, marketing executive, etc, will this particular job be the right next step?

To give you some real-life examples:

- **The job might interest you but do you actually want to work for this company?** You don't want to be like David who said yes to a job that was a two-hour journey each way. He started in July and it wasn't too bad, but as winter approached he had to start getting up at 5am, there were regular accidents and the traffic was heavy. He wasn't getting home till 9pm most evenings, meaning he was like an absent parent during the week. Added to that was the wear and tear on his car. He hadn't thought this through.

- **You might like the job but not the product.** Sally got offered a job as a marketing executive. She was delighted as it was a promotion, but she didn't like working for a drinks company, as whilst the money was good the nature of the work didn't match with her personal values.

- **The job is focused on skills you would rather not use.** Whilst Vicky was able to use Excel, it wasn't the skill she most enjoyed using. The recruitment consultancy company had 'sold' her to the company as an expert. Whilst delighted to be shortlisted she knew she did not have the level of expertise they sought and was quite nervous about the interview. Plus, even if she got the job she wouldn't want to be using this skill as the main focus of her job.

Review why you are going to be perfect for the job

If you want the job you must put a high level of effort into your preparation. You can't go half-heartedly into the interview or assessment centre – you will be wasting your time, and the time of the interviewer(s).

Think about *you*, and remind yourself why you will be great for the job. Re-read the advertisement, application form and letters and assess what you have to offer, i.e. your relevant strengths, experience and skills.

Asking yourself the following questions will help with this. Taking into account what you know about the job role, think through your responses:

- What qualifications do I have, what jobs or assignments have I done, and which achievements of mine fit with what I know of the position?

- What other unique selling points do I have in relation to this appointment?

- In which areas do I not seem to fit the job description, and might expect to be questioned accordingly?

- How will I deal with these questions?

- Will this be the right job for me?

- Why am I interested in this position?

- Why am I interested in this organisation?

You should have already thought through the answers to these questions before you applied for the job. Even if you did, it is worth considering them once more to make absolutely sure how you match up.

Find out as much as you can about the company

You will have already done some research to help you put your application together but you now need to do more. One of the more crucial tasks is to ascertain whether it is a company that is growing, and not a business in trouble.

A company's website is going to paint a positive picture, with the press releases and news pages talking about how well the company is doing. But are they? Before you give up a job you want to make sure that the job you are moving to will still exist in a few years time, or at least the experience gained will be valuable. So alongside reviewing the company website do an internet search and see what's being said about them. You also need to delve a bit deeper. The company might be doing well, but, for example, if they are in manufacturing or distribution, what about the industry they are supplying to?

You don't want to say yes to a new job and leave a secure position to find yourself being made redundant within a year. This is what recently happened to a client of mine called Roger, who now finds himself unemployed, very concerned about his future and full of regret for not foreseeing this.

As you find out more about the company, also find out more about the company's values. These are often listed on their website. Here, for instance are Microsoft's company values:

- A passion for technology

- Respectful and open

- Accountable

- Honest and with integrity

- Self-critical

- Eager to take on big challenges

Source: www.microsoft.com/uk/careers/values.mspx

You can then look for ways to demonstrate these values. If you were applying to Microsoft you would want to think of examples of being eager to take on big challenges and being accountable. Reading through the company values can also help you be sure that it is a company you want to work for.

Do your research on the industry

How much do you really know about the industry you are applying to? Reading up on your industry demonstrates that you can be strategic; you look beyond your job to consider issues relevant to the bigger picture. You can explore this more through reading professional journals, business pages of newspapers, dedicated websites, etc.

Research so you can ask intelligent questions

Many interviewers will ask the question, 'What do you know about us?' Employers want applicants who have had the initiative, courtesy and enthusiasm to find out something about their organisation. It matters less what specific information you found; the key is that you took the time to research the company. The more senior the position you seek, the more important the research becomes. You also need to look beyond the obvious and sometimes asking someone else to review the company website can help.

> Anna was applying for a job in medical sales and as we did an interview coaching session we discussed her research I did a search on the company website. The medical information went over my head but I did notice that they had introduced a range of beauty products. It wasn't on the main news page but a couple of levels down on the website, something caught my eye and I followed through and found details. It resulted in an interesting question for Anna to ask, and something that she had missed as she had focused on the technical detail.

Typical areas to research include:

- The organisation's recent history, competitors and market performance
- Any developments at industry levels, which may have affected the company
- Their range of products, goods or services
- Markets and market shares at home and overseas
- Business purpose and aims (mission statement)
- Future strategy
- Stated or inferred opportunities, problems or developments the company is facing

You can find out more from the company website, business sites such as www.ft.com, and through searching the internet. It's good to read what is being said in the business press and to study public views on open sites.

> You will gain a competitive edge if you can demonstrate your knowledge of the industry you are applying for – not just knowledge of the role you have applied for.

Think about what might be included in the assessment centre

Understanding what's required to be successful in the job can help you to think about what might be assessed at an assessment centre. For example, if you are applying for a graduate Fast Stream job with the civil service, expect to be assessed on writing policy papers; apply for a job as a consultant and you'll be assessed on your ability to run a consultancy meeting; or in PR to write press releases at short notice.

You should do this preparation even if it is 'just' an interview as you will still need to provide examples of your skills and experience.

This book will help you to 'get into role' and help you to identify what is likely to be assessed at the centre.

Research to give you a psychological advantage

The letter should tell you who will be interviewing you, and if it doesn't you can contact the company to find out. You can then find out what you can about the interviewer(s) via the company website, social networking sites and a general internet search.

The more you can find out, the better you can prepare. Subjects could include:

- Conferences they have spoken at
- Articles they have written
- Their progression through the company
- Possibly their hobbies and interests

All of this can help put you at an advantage. You can have read about what they have written, and perhaps include examples that tie in with their interests. There may even be a connection that you can exploit, but you must be subtle in your approach.

A word of caution: you must keep things real. You can't claim an avid interest in golf just because they are passionate about this hobby, as the conversation may move onto some specific details that would trip you up.

Notify the company if you have any special needs

If you have a disability such as visual impairment, dyslexia or you use a wheelchair, let the company know so they can make suitable arrangements. If you need things in large print, this can be arranged, but it is much harder to organise on the day. If you have dyslexia the timetable may need to be revised to give you additional time.

Please don't think that a disability will be held against you. The Disability Discrimination Act (DDA) 1995 makes it unlawful to discriminate against any person with a disability and employers have a duty to make reasonable adjustments to both selection procedures and on the job.

Review any feedback you have received from previous assessment centres

If you have previously attended an assessment centre you should have been given feedback on how you did, including your strengths, weaknesses and suggestions for development. It will be helpful to re-read this so you can take it into account.

Review your listening skills

If you are at an assessment centre there will be many times when you need to listen to others, such as in the group discussion, but also in the presentation and other exercises and when listening to instructions.

Active listening means also listening to the tone of voice, and the emphasis; *how* something is said is as important as what is said. It means taking turns to speak, waiting for a suitable time to speak, and not interrupting others. It also means looking for different ways of disagreeing, not being overly challenging and disparaging of others but saying something like, 'That's an interesting point, what makes you say that?' Or 'An alternative way of looking at this is xyz, what do others think of that?'

A word on a page lacks emphasis. When someone says 'yes', is this a sullen yes, a supportive yes, or something else? There are verbal and non-verbal behaviours that can reinforce what you want to say. You can demonstrate that you are listening by leaning forward, nodding your head in support and saying 'uh-huhs' etc.

Ensure you pay full attention to others by taking account of their gestures and body language and look at them when they are talking. As preparation you can practise summarising conversations and asking other people if you have accurately outlined the discussion.

Developing good listening skills is helpful, both at the recruitment stage and throughout your work and personal life.

Psychometric Testing

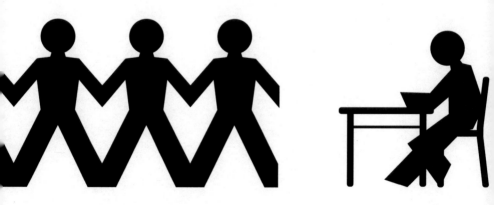

Chapter 3. Introducing psychometric tests

Psychometric testing has been used by large companies for over 30 years and the number of companies using them is growing, so let's make sure you understand what they are, why they are used and how you can increase your chances of doing well.

The standard interview is notorious for the biases that may influence an interviewer's decision. Interviewers may have prejudices against particular personality characteristics, thoughts about a particular gender or age and they are affected by their own mood and health. Against all of this psychometric testing is a much more objective way of assessing people. These type of tests are almost always included within an assessment centre.

Candidates often worry, and when we worry we don't do our best, so my aim is to take away some of the mystery and to get you ready through practical guidance and practice tests.

What is a psychometric test and how do they work?

Psychometric tests are a scientific way of measuring performance. There are two types:

1. **Maximum performance,** based on tests that have right and wrong answers (ability testing).

2. Tests of **typical performance** which indicate what a person is likely to do, or would prefer to do. These include personality questionnaires and assessments of motivation and emotional intelligence.

Tests of maximum performance come with strict time limits and you need to work fast but also be accurate. The tests are designed so that on average people in the relevant group would get about 50% of the answers right, and are designed so that most people won't complete the test.

Both tests are designed so that the instructions are clearly written, everyone has the same amount of time (for a timed ability test) and your scores are compared to other people so you know if you are above average, average or below average.

The most typical ability tests used in recruitment measure numerical and verbal reasoning, but you could face spatial reasoning tests if you are applying for a job in engineering or as an air traffic controller, and very specific tests if you are applying for a job as a computer programmer or a job where you need to learn a language.

Some companies will use ability tests as an initial sift when they get a very large number of applicants. For example, if you apply for a job as a graduate entrant on the civil service Fast Stream programme the psychometric testing results are used, alongside other evidence, to decide who goes on to the next stage of the selection process. **Other companies will use ability tests as part of an assessment centre.**

Tests need to be valid, reliable and fair

Validity is concerned with the extent that a test measures what it sets out to measure. So in recruitment if a test is meant to identify those with sales potential, over time the people who score highest should be those with the best sales performance.

Reliability is the extent that a test produces reliable results. A psychometric test should have a reliability of 0.8-0.9 where 1.0 means 100% reliability. It means that if someone took the test on several occasions the results would be similar (psychologists use statistics to take account of the effect of practice).

A test can be reliable without being valid. If every time I got on the scales I weighed 120 pounds that is a reliable measure, but if I know I actually weigh 150 pounds it is not a valid result.

The concept of **fairness** means that the test should not discriminate unfairly between people, due to reasons of age, sex, race, etc.

Testing used to be done in a large meeting room with a test administrator but nowadays many companies use online testing facilities. Whether testing is done online or at a centre you should be given details in advance including a practice test. This is good practice on the company's part, but I know only too well that not all companies will do this, so the guidance in this and subsequent chapters is going to help.

Test interpretation

When you take a psychometric test your results are compared against other people who do a job similar to the role you are applying for. This is known as a 'norm group' which is a group of people who have previously taken the test. So for one particular test the norm groups could include graduates, bank managers or engineers. The assessment centre designer would have made sure that they not only chose the most appropriate test, but that there is also a relevant norm group, as they can't get you to take a test if there is no relevant comparison group.

Once your score is compared to a relevant group it becomes much more meaningful. For example, if on a particular test you have scored 18 out of 30, what does that mean? Once your score is compared to a norm group it is much more relevant. For example, compared to the UK general population, your score could be in the 75th percentile (your score is in the top 25%) or compared to top executives you might be in the bottom 25th percentile. It's far more useful to know how your score compares to others than to have a raw score.

Can I fail a test?

Tests are not thought of as pass or fail as scores are usually presented as percentiles. So a score at the 60th percentile does not mean a score of 60%, it means you scored better than 60% of a comparable group. When you get your results you might be given the score, e.g. the 60th percentile, but your results are more likely to be shown as a number or letter with different scores falling into different bands, such as A-E where C would be average.

If the psychometric testing is the first stage of a selection process, then there will be a cut-off point and if you fall below this you will not go through to the next stage.

When a company makes a decision over who gets the job offer, final decisions are made based on an analysis of all the data – tests, interview and other assessment-centre exercises – so you may not score highly on an ability test, but if you do well everywhere else you could still be in with a chance as the company will want to take all of your strengths into account. There is more information on decision making in the assessment centre section.

Online testing

Online testing is taking over from the old-style paper and pencil tests, but companies can be concerned about candidates taking timed ability tests at home. What's to stop a candidate getting someone else to sit their test? Or a group of people taking a test together, thus getting improbably high scores?

To counter possible fraud some companies get candidates to go to a venue for the online testing, particularly with large-scale recruitment. Other companies are introducing randomised item banks that comprise far more questions than is needed for one particular test. This means that every test can contain a different selection of questions but will be equally valid as the questions are taken at random from the same large database.

Other companies will allow people to take the assessment online but if the candidate reaches the next stage they face the chance of being asked to take a second test under secure conditions. This time a similar but different version would be used. If the results are not similar you would not get through this stage. One test publisher asks candidates to complete an 'honesty contract' where the candidate is warned that they might be asked to retake the assessment in a secure environment. No one knows if they will be retested.

An additional benefit to the company using online testing is that additional data can be collected, such as automatically adjusting the complexity of the questions. If you get the first few questions correct the test can jump to more complex questions. The test can also collect data on how quickly you answer each question.

Invite to take the tests

You will receive a letter or email explaining that you need to take psychometric tests as part of your application for a job. This letter should include details on the particular tests you will take, for example tests of numerical and verbal reasoning; why you are being asked to take them; how they will be administered; are when and where, i.e. online, from home or at a testing session as part of an assessment centre visit.

> The invite should include some practice tests. Read this information carefully so you fully understand what you need to do. When you complete the practice questions don't just check you got the right answer but be clear why it was the right answer, as this will be very useful when you do the test for real.

Many companies will tell you the actual name of the test, and this should be included in the practice materials. You can then do a search on the internet to find out more details, including perhaps further practice material. Occasionally a company will not send you further details. If not ask for it, as it is good practice for a company to provide details on the tests you will take.

> If you are told that you will be undertaking psychometric testing make sure you find out further details about the specific tests.

If you are to take the test at home you will need use of a computer with internet access where you can work in peace, so not at a library or your place of work. Any computer bought in the last few years will be fine (for older computers you may want to check they are okay).

If you are likely to have any problems, let the company know so that alternative arrangements can be made.

It's not possible to have copies of the actual test to practice as the validity of the test could be compromised. So do complete the practice tests in subsequent chapters and follow the links to online sites which offer further practice materials.

> ## The British Psychological Society
>
> The British Psychological Society sets the standards for test administration and use, and the people involved in selection, administration and feedback will have signed up to user guidelines and a code of practice, alongside relevant training. This includes Level A, which covers the knowledge and skills needed to administer, use and interpret ability tests, and Level B which covers personality testing. Read more at www.psychtesting.org.uk.

Candidates with disabilities

The Disability Discrimination Act (1995) makes it unlawful for an employer to treat a disabled person less favourably than a fully abled person. If you have a disability or feel that you might need special arrangements, let the company know as soon as possible so that specific arrangements can be made. For a candidate with dyslexia this may mean that the instructions are read out to you rather than you reading them to yourself. A candidate with a visual impairment could get large print materials, or more major adjustments might need to be made. The company will consult a chartered psychologist for specific advice.

Test administration

Tests are generally provided under controlled or supervised administration. Controlled administration is the method used for online testing. The software will have been designed so that it covers all the questions and answers that would be asked in a supervised session. Supervised administration is the 'traditional' method where people take the test under the supervision of a test administrator.

For a paper and pencil test the instructions will be read out to you; this is to ensure that every group gets told what to do in exactly the same way. For online testing the instructions will be read on the screen, and sometimes there are voice instructions as well. You will be reminded of the purpose of the test, and how long it will take. You almost always get some example questions to work through first of all, and you will be told the answers, but make sure you understand how the answers were arrived at.

> If you attend a supervised testing session make sure you go to the toilet beforehand as you can't leave the room whilst the test is underway. If taking a test at home, you still need to remain at your computer during the test as the test comes with an inbuilt clock.

Internet testing

You will be sent details by email including your user ID and password, along with the address of the relevant website. When you log on you will be taken through a series of instructions to make sure that you are clear on what needs to be done.

Read the instructions carefully; sometimes you need to disable firewalls and anti-virus software to ensure the programme runs correctly. Make sure all other applications and programs are closed. This does include such applications as the Weather Bug, Lotus Notes, animated screensavers, and all e-mail programs. It also includes any application in the background that may be refreshing.

Make sure that you will not be disturbed, keep family members and pets out of the room, switch your mobile off and unplug the house phone.

Preparation for a testing session

I've taken many ability tests in my career history; every single time I went for a promotion when working for the Post Office I'd sit another test. What was helpful was to do some warm-up exercises. I used a really old copy of Hans Eysenck's *Test Your IQ* as it got me into the right frame of mind for test taking, even if I was practicing intelligence tests rather than verbal and numerical reasoning tests. Just as a marathon runner goes training, so a candidate should practice taking tests under timed conditions. Reading this section gives you a good overview, but for the best preparation you should look to take as many tests as you can. The following chapters provide details and examples, and links to practice tests are included at the end of this chapter. **It doesn't matter that the tests differ, it is getting you into the right mindset to take timed tests that is important.**

The best thing to do in final preparation for a psychometric test is to **get a good night's sleep the night before and try to relax.** Ideally, you will be in top form before you do a test but if you are ill or something has happened (perhaps a bereavement or accident) then you may be able to reschedule, but this isn't always possible. Under these circumstances be sure to tell the test administrator about your personal situation.

> Practice really helps, so read this chapter (and the other chapters in this section) carefully. It's a great help to practice psychometric tests, as becoming more familiar with them reduces anxiety and practising under time constraints accustoms you to the requirements of a test. Don't forget to use the online sites listed at the end of this chapter for further practice.

Now for the obvious:

1. If you wear glasses, make sure you take them with you to the venue and wear them when you take the test.

2. Make sure you know where you are going and get there in plenty of time.

3. Take along a calculator just in case you are allowed to use one

At the venue:

4. Accept you could be nervous and treat the nerves as the adrenaline that will help you to perform well.

5. Keep calm and do some deep breathing.

6. Be comfortable. Take off your jacket and slip off your shoes if that helps, but make sure you can put them back on quickly.

7. Listen carefully to the instructions and ask questions if anything isn't clear.

8. You will get a chance to do some example questions at the beginning, and **if you don't understand anything make sure you ask**. You will be told the correct answer for these; if you don't understand how the answer was arrived at, again do ask.

9. As the test starts, read each question carefully so you are clear about what you need to do.

10. If you don't know an answer you can provide your best choice, but don't guess wildly. Sometimes you will be penalised for an incorrect answer, but not always. It's best to ask if this is the case.

11. Work at a brisk pace but don't race or you could make avoidable mistakes.

12. If there is paper available you can use it to make calculations.

13. Follow the instructions. If you happen to get a paper and pencil test do use X and not a tick if that's what is required, or completely shade in a O and not tick if that is what is asked for.

14. With a paper and pencil test, if you make corrections make it clear which is the correct one.

15. With some questions, when you don't know the answer you might find it easier to eliminate some and see what is left.

16. Tests often get more difficult as they progress so don't allocate the same amount of time to each question.

17. Look away from the test occasionally, it can help your concentration.

18. Don't be worried if other people are working faster than you, it doesn't mean they are getting the answers right!

19. Keep track of the time, write the start time down on a piece of paper and position your watch so you can easily see the clock face.

20. Don't expect to complete the tests. They are designed so that the average person doesn't finish.

21. Don't give up if you think you are performing poorly, we're often not good judges of our own performance.

22. If you have some free time at the end of the test, go back and review your answers.

Test feedback

You will have an interview with a psychologist or psychometrician to discuss the results. If this is just to discuss the ability tests this could be quite short, but may last for an hour or longer if it includes discussing a personality questionnaire.

When you get the feedback, if you don't understand something, ask. The British Psychological *Society's Code of Good Practice in Psychological Testing* says:

> Provide the test taker and other authorised persons with feedback about the results in a form that makes clear the implications of the results, is clear and in a style appropriate to their level of understanding.

So you should be able to understand the format, and if not or if you need more information do ask for clarification.

People take different approaches to tests. Some people like to work quickly, and don't check anything till they have finished and will then go back through their answers. More people will work at a slower pace, checking answers, sometimes twice. When I give feedback to candidates I'll also ask them about the approach they took and check their results. Some candidates might be slow, but with a high level of accuracy – which is more important for some jobs.

How to improve

Over the longer term, your performance **may** improve by doing the following:

- Reading newspapers, reports and business journals (may improve your verbal skills for verbal tests)

- Solving crosswords (may help verbal problem solving)

- Reading financial reports in newspapers, studying tables of data, doing number calculations and puzzles without a calculator (may help numerical skills)

- Checking details in the paper (could improve checking skills)

- Looking at objects in various ways and angles (could develop spatial skills)

- Looking at flow charts and diagrams (should improve diagramming skills)

- Playing chess or Tantrix (will help develop diagrammatic reasoning skills)

- If you are applying for a job that has its own technical terminology, be familiar with the different terms

Further help

You can undertake practice tests on various websites. I particularly like the ones from Kent University (www.kent.ac.uk/careers/psychotests.htm) which provide practice aptitude tests for a number of areas: numerical reasoning, logical reasoning, spatial ability, verbal reasoning and much more.

Special gift for all readers from Team Focus Ltd, who kindly provided testing materials for use in this book

You can sample a range of full-length tests and questionnaires for free and receive a personalised report. This includes a verbal reasoning test, the Emotional Intelligence questionnaire, Resilience Scale and Values-based Indicator of Motivation.

Please go to: www.profilingforsuccess.com, click on the 'more' button under the 'Taking an Assessment' box and follow the online instructions. You will be prompted to enter the following codes:

Client code: pfs

Access code: develop

Password: pfsdevelop

Continue through the screens, entering biographical data when prompted and the email address to which the feedback report is to be sent. This is normally sent within minutes of completing the tests. After each test is completed, you will be given the opportunity to complete another test.

Online testing sites

www.criterionpartnership.co.uk/test_samples For verbal and numerical sample tests. This is from Criterion Partnership, who kindly provided testing materials for use in this book.
www.shldirect.com www.shl.com For further details and practice tests. SHL Group Ltd kindly provided testing materials for use in this book.
www.talentlens.co.uk/resources.aspx This is the Pearson Assessment site which kindly provided details on the Watson-Glaser Critical Thinking Assessment. The information here is available to test users.
www.savilleconsulting.com/products/aptitude_preparationguides.aspx Saville Consulting provide a series of guides to help you prepare.
www.faststream.gov.uk If you are thinking of applying for the civil service Fast Stream you can access some practice tests once you have registered.
http://practicetests.cubiks.com Another site to take practice tests on, from a test publisher.
http://careers.jpmorgan.com/student/jpmorgan/careers/europe/advice/test Practice tests from JP Morgan (banking and financial services).
www.kcpltd.com There are a number of practice tests you can take on this site, where you can also buy a test and get comprehensive feedback.
www.psychometrics-uk.com This site boasts specific tests for assessing computer programmers.
www.morrisby.com Choose practice tests from the left-hand menu.
www.assessmentday.co.uk Provides links so you can take practice numerical, verbal and inductive reasoning tests. There are some free examples and an option for a comprehensive online test at reasonable cost.

http://students.efinancialcareers.co.uk/numerical_test.htm   For further tests to practice numerical ability.
www.practicetests.co.uk   At the time of writing this only has an option to take a sales test, but there is a lot of detail on psychometrics if the subject interests you.
www.diagonalthinking.co.uk   This test has been created to see if you are suitable for a career in advertising.
http://bit.ly/gG4fm via www.psychtesting.org.uk   The British Psychological Society *Test-Takers guide*.
www.mensa.org.uk   For IQ tests.
www.bbc.co.uk/skillswise   To practice maths techniques such as subtraction, multiplication, division, rations and percentages
www.mymaths.co.uk   To revise your maths skills

This chapter has introduced you to psychometric testing. In the next four chapters you can read about, and practice, a number of different timed ability tests and also read more about personality questionnaires.

All these links are available online at:
www.amazingpeople.co.uk/shortlisted.html.

Chapter 4. Verbal reasoning and critical-thinking tests

There are a number of verbal reasoning tests and some are more complex than others. It's the role of the psychologist to choose the tests which are at the right level for the job being recruited for.

A verbal reasoning or critical thinking test measures how well someone can understand, evaluate and manipulate information that is presented in written form. It's an essential ability for many jobs, and hence this type of assessment is very popular in recruitment.

Many people think that they have good verbal reasoning skills, and are disappointed when they get the results from their assessment. This chapter contains a number of example questions so you can practice. You can then read some key tips to help you to improve.

Tests of critical reasoning/thinking

There are many tests of verbal critical reasoning, such as the Watson Glaser Critical Thinking Appraisal, the SHL Verbal Critical Reasoning test, Utopia from Criterion Partnership and many more. With the majority of these tests you are given a paragraph followed by a series of questions, to which you have to choose the right answer. For example:

With thanks to SHL Group Ltd

The image above shows a comprehensive piece of text, a statement and three options. You then have to make a choice: is the statement true, false or is there insufficient evidence to say? The instructions tell you to base your answers only on the information given in the passage, but this is easier said than done! Some of the paragraphs will contain information that you have a view on and it is tempting to make your decision based as well on information that you know but is irrelevant to the exercise.

The answer to this question is 'True'. The paragraph says 'promoting the interests of the organisation often conflicts with their own best interests'.

There is usually a set amount of time to do this, for example 48 questions to be answered in 25 minutes.

> The timescales are designed to be stretching and there is always a time/accuracy trade off. If you aren't sure, then you can give your best choice, but it is usually best to avoid wild guessing.

Usually, you get time to read the instructions so you understand what needs to be done before the test starts properly, but not always. If you are asked to take the Watson-Glaser Critical Thinking Appraisal you will find that reading the instructions on what to do is part of the overall test and so must be done with in your time allowance, although you should have received a practice leaflet in advance.

The Watson-Glaser test differs from other critical reasoning tests as there are five different types of test all contained within the assessment:

1. The first one measures **Inference** – the conclusion you can draw from certain facts. We can infer things and these may be true, or not. The answer is not always black or white. Though whilst some answers will be clear, others will be less so and for this test there is a five point scale: true, partly true, partly false and false with a middle option of insufficient data.

2. The second test is **Recognition of Assumptions** and from a statement you need to say whether an assumption is true or false.

3. The third test is concerned with **Deduction**; can you draw a conclusion, or not, based on your reading of a statement?

4. Test four is concerned with **Interpretation** and asks you to again look at a paragraph and interpret the data, and say whether you can draw a conclusion from it.

5. The final test is concerned with **Evaluation of Arguments**. You read the statement, look at the proposed argument and make a judgement, stating if this judgement is strong or weak.

This particular test is sometimes timed, at other times you can continue till you finish.

EXAMPLE

Statement:
Two hundred school students in their early teens voluntarily attended a recent weekend student conference in Leeds. At this conference, the topics of race relations and means of achieving lasting world peace were discussed, since these were problems that the students selected as being most vital in today's world.

Proposed Inferences:

Test 1

1. As a group, the students who attended this conference showed a keener interest in broad social problems than do most other people in their early teens. (PT, because, as is common knowledge, most people in their early teens do not show so much serious concern with broad social problems. It cannot be considered definitely true from the facts given because these facts do not tell how much concern other young teenagers may have. It is also possible that some of the students volunteered to attend mainly because they wanted a weekend outing.)

	T	PT	ID	PF	F
1	○	✕	○	○	○

2. The majority of the students had not previously discussed the conference topics in the schools. (PF, because the students' growing awareness of these topics probably stemmed at least in part from discussions with teachers and classmates.)

	T	PT	ID	PF	F
2	○	○	○	✕	○

3. The students came from all parts of the country. (ID, because there is no evidence for this inference.)

	T	PT	ID	PF	F
3	○	○	✕	○	○

4. The students discussed mainly industrial relations problems. (F, because it is given in the statement of facts that the topics of race relations and means of achieving world peace were the problems chosen for discussion.)

	T	PT	ID	PF	F
4	○	○	○	○	✕

5. Some teenage students felt it worthwhile to discuss problems of race relations and ways of achieving world peace. (T, because this inference follows from the given facts; therefore it is true.)

	T	PT	ID	PF	F
5	✕	○	○	○	○

With thanks to Pearson Assessments

Let's have a look at a typical instruction page, so you can see the sort of information you will get.

Verbal reasoning

Instructions

The verbal reasoning test looks at your ability to think logically about written information. You will see passages of text, followed by statements relating to the text. You have to read each passage of text carefully and then decide whether each statement follows logically from the information in the passage. For each statement there are three answer options you can choose from: true, false or can't tell.

True	This means that, on the basis of the information in the passage, the statement is true or logically follows from the passage.
False	This means that, on the basis of the information in the passage, the statement is false.
Can't tell	This means that you cannot tell from the information in the passage whether the statement is true or false.

When deciding on whether a statement is true, false or you can't tell, it is important to base your answer only on the information in the passage and not on any other knowledge you may have. Your task is simply to judge whether or not the statement follows logically from the passage.

Have a look at this practice question. The answer to the first statement is given. Try and work out the answers to the other three statements, and then check your answers against the explanations at the end of this chapter.

Example

The word 'weather' is used to describe the day-to-day changes in our atmosphere. The source of these changes is the sun. As the Earth spins at an angle to the sun, areas around the equator get more heat from the sun than other areas. Land also absorbs more heat than the sea.

The atmosphere tries to equalise these differences in temperature, moving hot air that is near the equator to colder areas near the North and South Pole, and cool air to warmer areas. This movement of air is also affected by the spinning of the Earth and friction between the air and land. This process creates areas of high and low pressure in the atmosphere that result in the weather we experience on the ground.

The first statement has been answered, and you can see the result and the reason why. Now have a go at statements 2, 3 and 4. You can check your results at the end of this chapter.

1. Warm air tends to move towards the equator.

    The answer to this question is False. The passage tells us that the atmosphere moves 'hot air that is near the equator to colder areas near the North and South Pole' and 'cool air to warmer areas'. Warmer air therefore moves away from the equator, not towards it.

2. The sea cools down more quickly than land.

3. The sun causes changes in the weather.

4. Areas of high pressure are more common around the equator.

These tests are measuring your ability to reason, not checking your knowledge, so only focus on the information in the test and do not use any prior information you have, as it might trip you up. Most of the topics discussed are generally topics which should be unfamiliar to you, so you can concentrate on the information given, rather than using prior knowledge.

> A good way of approaching these tests is to skim read the text and then go through it more carefully as you answer each question.

When you do a test for real, you will either choose an answer from a screen, for an online test, or put your answers onto a separate answer sheet if it is a paper and pencil test. In this case you must make sure that the number of the question you are answering corresponds with the number on the answer sheet.

TASK

Let's now look at a further four examples. I suggest you work your way through these, attempting all of the examples.

Each piece of text is followed by some questions. Choose the one you think is right, continue till you have completed all four tests, and then you can check your answers at the end of the book and come back to the ones you got wrong.

Verbal meaning test 1

Utopia guides to greener living

Losing my emissions – the future of green motoring

Do catalytic converters prevent pollution?

Whilst catalytic converters don't actually prevent pollution, they do help to cut it down. Their purpose is to convert the poisonous carbon monoxide gas, and other pollutants produced by cars into carbon dioxide. They don't, however, work to full effect on short car journeys, since they only work once they have been warmed up.

Are electric cars greener?

This is entirely dependent on how the electricity is generated. The electricity generated from the burning of coal, for example, is likely to have high emissions of pollution. On the other hand, electricity generated by nuclear power will have less emissions of harmful gases than an ordinary petrol or diesel car. Electric cars, are also problematical because they need heavy and expensive batteries, which need to be frequently recharged. They are not so good for travelling long distances.

Is diesel a cleaner fuel than petrol?

This is a complicated issue because the emissions produced by a diesel car are different to those produced by a petrol car, and much depends on how well a car is maintained. Some diesel cars might actually give off more harmful gases than petrol cars.

Is it better for the environment to use biofuels?

This is not really the case because they give off less energy per quantity than ordinary fuels. There is also the environmental cost of producing biofuels; intensive farming of the crops, fertilizers and pesticides used on them, and then the conversion of the crops into the fuels. Biofuels emit less sulphur than conventional fuels, but they do produce more nitrogen monoxide. Biofuels can have a negative effect on the environment.

What about future developments in fuel technology?

Hydrogen is often cited as the way forward for green motoring, with fuel-cell technology producing only water as a waste product. Although hydrogen is the most common element in the universe it requires complex processes for its production, storage and distribution. Nuclear powered cars are really only suitable for time travel (which requires 1.21 **gigawatts** of electricity).

1. Catalytic converters are most effective in reducing pollution when cars are used for short journeys.

The statement is **True** from the information given	The statement is **False** from the information given	**Cannot Say** for certain from the information given whether the statement is true or false.

2. Diesel cars generally emit smaller quantities of harmful gases than petrol cars.

The statement is **True** from the information given	The statement is **False** from the information given	**Cannot Say** for certain from the information given whether the statement is true or false.

3. Cars without catalytic converters produce poisonous substances.

The statement is **True** from the information given	The statement is **False** from the information given	**Cannot Say** for certain from the information given whether the statement is true or false.

4. On balance, biofuels are more environmentally safe than ordinary fuels.

The statement is **True** from the information given	The statement is **False** from the information given	**Cannot Say** for certain from the information given whether the statement is true or false.

5. There is an abundant supply of hydrogen available.

The statement is **True** from the information given	The statement is **False** from the information given	**Cannot Say** for certain from the information given whether the statement is true or false.

With thanks to Criterion Partnership Ltd

Verbal meaning test 2

This exercise consists of a passage of text followed by several statements. You have to read the text and then decide whether the statements are True, False or whether you Cannot say whether they are True or False. Your responses must be based on the text in the passage. Indicate your response by placing an X in the box next to your choice (True, False or Cannot say).

Radar was used originally by ships to detect icebergs and other obstacles. A radar system transmits radio waves and listens for any echoes. By analysing the reflected signal, the reflector can be located and sometimes identified. Distance is measured by the time it takes the pulse to travel to and from the target.

Most radars operate at frequencies from about 220 MHz to 35 GHz. However, some radars have operated as high as 5 MHz and others at 94 GHz. Usually the higher the frequency, the sharper the return signal and the more accuracy can be obtained in determining distance and location.

1. Radar enables all objects at sea to be identified. ☐ True ☐ False ☐ Cannot say

2. Radar operating at higher frequencies is usually more accurate. ☐ True ☐ False ☐ Cannot say

3. Radar is only used to detect objects at sea. ☐ True ☐ False ☐ Cannot say

With thanks to Perception Business Psychologists

Verbal meaning test 3

Instructions

This exercise is about understanding the meaning of words.

Each question consists of five words, four of these words are similar in some way; they may have the same meaning, same use or same properties. Your task is to find the word that does not fit with the other four.

Once you have decided on the word that does not fit with the others indicate your response by placing a cross in the box A, B, C, D, or E.

A. Apple	B. Orange	C. Pear	D. Potato	E. Mango
A. Run	B. Walk	C. Swim	D. Jog	E. Skip

A. ☐   B. ☐   C. ☐   D. ☐   E. ☐

A. ☐   B. ☐   C. ☐   D. ☐   E. ☐

With thanks to Perception Business Psychologists

Checking test 4

Instructions

This exercise is a test of how well you can check the details of written material. You are given a Master List of stock items and their stock number; next to this is a second list that has been copied from the Master List.

Your task is to check that the details in the Copy List are exactly the same as those in the Master List.

If they are the same, then place an X in the box for 'correct', if the details are not the same, then place an X in the appropriate box to show whether there is a mistake in the Item Name, Stock Number or Name and Stock Number.

Master List		Copy List					
Name	Stock Number	Name	Stock Number	Correct	Name	Number	Name and Number
Overalls	123574	Ovaralls	123574	☐	☐	☐	☐
Chairs	214658	Chairs	214658	☐	☐	☐	☐
Tea cups	321957	Tea cups	312957	☐	☐	☐	☐

With thanks to Perception Business Psychologists

Check your answers now against those at the back of the book. You can then come back and look again at the ones you got wrong.

I've concentrated on verbal reasoning tests as they are the most popular for professional and managerial positions, however you might also find some others such as spelling tests or word meaning tests.

Verbal speed tests

Verbal speed tests tend to be used more when recruiting at administrative and clerical level, but you may still face these at graduate and professional level. The tests could be of grammar, spelling and checking and often require a good understanding of the meaning of words, so if English is your second language you could be at a disadvantage.

Spelling speed tests

There are two main spelling speed tests. They both involve picking out the incorrectly spelt word. Sometimes this is out of a row of words where one is spelt correctly and the other 3 are not, and you have to choose the correct spelling. Another way is to give you a paragraph and you have to pick out the words which are spelt incorrectly. To practise and improve your spelling write down any words that you find difficult to spell.

Typical words include:

Separate	Success	Revision
Occurrence	Embarrassment	Inconvenience

Word meanings

This speed test gives you a choice of words and you have to say which is the right one to link with a word. For example:

Boy is to man as girl is to:			
Elephant	Woman	Children	Horse
Ocean is to pond as deep is to:			
Shallow	Well	Sea	Lake

With thanks to Perception Business Psychologists

Key tips

- Read the instructions carefully.

- Focus purely on the information in the text, and don't use any other knowledge you may have.

- The information will sometimes be above the questions, at other times it will be in a separate booklet. If this is the case, make sure you are looking at the right item.

- Manage your time so you can answer as many questions as possible.

- Completing crosswords and word puzzles will help.

- Make sure you understand any technical terms used in the industry you are applying to.

- Read a complex article, perhaps something from the *Financial Times* or *The Economist*, and summarise it using bullet points for key points, then re-check the article.

- Don't forget, when you get the invite to complete psychometric tests ask for details on the particular test you will sit. That way you can do further research online.

- There are many more tests that you can complete via online sites, see the section at the end of Chapter 3. You can also find all of these available at.
www.amazingpeople.co.uk/shortlisted.html

Answers

Answers and explanations to the practice questions

Q2. The answer to this question is **'Can't Tell'**. The passage tells us that "*Land also absorbs more heat than the sea*". It does not tell us anything about how quickly land and sea cools down. Although some people may know that land cools down more quickly than sea, this statement should not be answered 'False' as this information is not given in the passage. Remember, your answer should be based only on the information in the passage and not any other knowledge you have.

Q3. The answer to this question is **'True'**. The first sentence tells us that "*weather is …the day-to-day changes in our atmosphere*". The second sentence says, "*The source of these changes is the sun*". Therefore the statement is true from the information in the passage.

Q4. The answer to this question is **'Can't Tell'**. The passage states that the movement of air "*… creates areas of high and low pressure …*". It also tells us that areas around the equator tend to be warmer, and that warm air moves from the equator to cooler areas. However, the passage does not give any information about air pressure around the equator, so you cannot tell whether the statement is true or false.

Chapter 5. Numerical tests

Tests of numerical ability are mainly focused on your ability to solve problems. You are usually given charts, graphs or tables of data about which you are then questioned.

This is an important ability to possess as many jobs require people to be comfortable with figures, and not just in the obvious ones such as accountancy (where passing the accountancy qualification is sufficient evidence). In many jobs, from sales to management, you need to be able to make accurate judgements when you review numerical data.

Sometimes the test is focused more on the skill of using numbers than with how well you can reason. Many people have forgotten how to calculate percentages without a calculator and are not able to use their knowledge of adding, subtraction, multiplication and division in a problem-solving scenario.

A good way to prepare for numerical tests is to do some old-fashioned maths revision. You need to make sure that you are comfortable with adding, subtraction, multiplication, division, ratios and percentages. There is some great practice material at: www.bbc.co.uk/skillswise.

Let's begin by looking at two examples from the SHL online test site.

In each scenario you have to make one choice from five options. It's rare that the answer is obvious; you do need to do some thinking.

Example 1

shl			Test Progress		Minutes Remaining
					00

Bentrim Outsourcing - figures last year				
Offshore Resource		Outsourcing (UK)	Total time for completion of projects	
Region	Project Managers	Projects	Estimated time per project	Average time spent per project
Asia	19	13	325 hours	278 hours
Americas	10	6	372 hours	382 hours
Europe	6	4	274 hours	279 hours
Africa	6	7	127 hours	148 hours
Australia	2	3	302 hours	298 hours

Example 2

What is the average time spent per outsourced project, across all regions for all of the projects?

- 112 hours
- 271 hours
- 956 hours
- 8,952 hours
- 9,348 hours

Help   Next

With thanks to SHL Group Ltd

The question we are asked to answer is the average time spent per outsourced project across all regions for all of the projects. To calculate this, firstly we need to calculate the total amount of time spent on all projects and then divide that value by the total number of projects. To calculate the total number of hours spent on projects we need to multiply the number of projects (middle column) by the average time spent per project (right-hand column) for all regions. We then add these five numbers together to give the total time spent on projects for all regions. Doing this gives a total time of:

(13x278) + (6x382) + (4x279) + (7x148) + (3x298) = 8,952 hours

The total number of projects is 33 (13+6+4+7+3)

The average time for all projects across all regions is therefore 8,952 divided by 33 = 271.27

This can be truncated to 271 (the second answer)

Shortcuts

For those with good estimating skills, it is possible to choose the correct answer without doing any calculations at all. If the possible answers are reviewed, it can be seen that 112 hours is less than any of the average time spent per project values, and 956 hours is significantly higher than any of the values. Since the overall average has to be between the highest and lowest average time spent per project (382 hours and 148 hours) then the only possible answer is 271.

Example 2

shl®		Test Progress	Minutes Remaining
REDEFINE PERFORMANCE		▮▮▮▮▮▮▮▮	**00**

Question 1

Which mine can produce the greatest amount of units of electricity before it runs out of coal?

World Fossil Fuel Regulation			
UK Coal Energy			
UK Mines	Extraction (000s tonnes) per year	Electricity production per kg (units)	Remaining coal (millions of tonnes)
Folen	46,324	17.0	68.27
Dirme	34,953	12.3	70.95
lit	74,036	14.2	62.73
Ryken	13,684	21.0	61.02
All Others	385,306	14.7	82.63

- 1 tonne = 1,000 kilograms
- An average UK household utilises 4.5 units of electricity per day
- One unit of electricity is sold for £0.08

- ⬤ Folen
- ⬤ Dirme
- ⬤ lit
- ⬤ Ryken
- ⬤ All Others

Help   Next ▶

With thanks to SHL Group Ltd

The question we have to answer is which mine can produce the greatest amount of units of electricity before it runs out of coal. In order to answer this question, we need to work out how much electricity each mine can produce before it runs out of coal. We do this by multiplying the number of tonnes of coal remaining (far right column in table) by the electricity production per kg (second column from right). We also need to multiply the electricity production number by 1,000 to convert the electricity production into units per tonne rather than units per kg. The numbers come out at:

Folen: 1.16m units Dirme: 0.87m units Lit: 0.89m units Ryken: 1.28m units and All Others: 1.21m units.

On that basis, Ryken can produce the greatest amount of units of electricity before it runs out of coal.

Shortcuts

To save time and avoid doing so many calculations, you do not need to multiply by 1,000 to convert from kg to tonnes since the same factor is applied to all mines and therefore does not impact the end result. For those with good estimating skills, some of the mines can be eliminated. For example, Lit has a lower value for both electricity production and remaining coal than both All Others and Folen and so cannot produce the greatest amount. In the same way, Dirme cannot be higher than All Others. Therefore we really only need to calculate the remaining production for Folen, Ryken and All Others.

Let's now have a look at a typical instruction page, so you can see the sort of information you will get.

Numerical reasoning

Instructions

The numerical reasoning test looks at your ability to solve numerical problems. You will see some numerical information followed by questions that relate to the information. For each question you are given five possible answers. Calculators are not allowed in this numerical test.

Have a look at this practice question. The answer to the first question is given. Try and work out the answers to the other three questions, and then check your answers against the explanations at the end of this chapter.

This table shows the annual cost of breakdown cover with two motoring organisations:

	Motoring Organisation	
Type of cover	Blue Star	Green Arrow
Gold	£75	£90
Silver	£65	£60
Bronze	£40	£30

1. Three members of a family share equally the cost of Silver cover for one car with Green Arrow. How much does each person pay?

A. £20

B. £25

C. £30

D. £60

E. £180

The correct answer is £20. To answer this question you first have to find out how much Silver cover with Green Arrow costs. The table shows you that this is £60. To find the cost per person you have to divide £60 by 3. £60 divided equally between three people gives you the answer of £20.

2. There is a 10% discount if you take out breakdown cover for more than one car. What is the cost of having two cars with Green Arrow Bronze cover?

A. £46

B. £54

C. £60

D. £66

E. £72

3. What is the ratio of the cost of Silver cover with Green Arrow to Gold cover with Green Arrow?

A. 1:3

B. 2:3

C. 3:2

D. 2:1

E. 3:1

4. The cost of Bronze cover with Blue Star increases to £50. By what percentage has the cost of Bronze cover increased?

A. 10%

B. 20%

C. 25%

D. 50%

E. 125%

Of course the actual test will involve numbers presented in different ways, including tables, graphs and pie charts. You get a series of questions with a choice of around five answers; you then have to choose the right one. Only one is correct and often one is a very close second so you need to take time to work though the questions carefully.

TASK

Let's now look at a further three examples. I suggest you work your way through them, attempting all of them.

In each case you will see a chart, image or table followed by a choice of possible answers. Choose the one you think is right, continue till you have completed all three tests, and you can then check your answers at the end of the book and come back and look again at any that you got wrong.

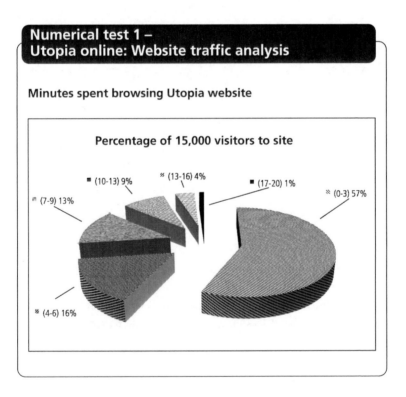

**Numerical test 1 –
Utopia online: Website traffic analysis**

Minutes spent browsing Utopia website

Percentage of 15,000 visitors to site

- (10-13) 9%
- (13-16) 4%
- (17-20) 1%
- (7-9) 13%
- (0-3) 57%
- (4-6) 16%

Utopia online site traffic statistics

Year	Number of visitors	Average number of pages visited
Year 1 (Launch)	50,248	1.25
Year 2	72,811	1.25
Year 3	97,309	1.5
Year 4	127,726	1.75
Year 5	153,436	2
Year 6	182,374	2.25
Year 7 (Last year)	210,478	2.5

1. What was the average number of visitors per month in the first 3 years after launch?

A	B	C	D	E
4,187	6,121	18,364	55,092	73,456

2. How many of the site visitors spent 3 minutes or less browsing? (Note: give your answer as a number of visitors, not a percentage.)

A	B	C	D	E
2,400	6,450	8,000	8,550	10,950

3. Based on the information given, what would you forecast the average number of pages visited to be in year 10?

A	B	C	D	E
2.50	2.75	3.00	3.25	3.50

4. What percentage of visitors spent between 4 and 13 minutes browsing the site?

A	B	C	D	E
9%	13%	16%	26%	38%

5. If the total number of visitors is 210,478, estimate how many browsed the site for less than 10 minutes. (Note: give your answer as a number of readers, not a percentage.)

A	B	C	D	E
12,900	29,467	181,011	199,954	210,478

Numerical test 2

This exercise is about practical calculations.

Instructions

In these examples your are asked to work out the answer to the question and then place an X in the square next to your chosen answer, A, B, C, D, or E. All the questions in this exercise have been designed so that you should not need a calculator, but you may use a pen and paper for making any calculations.

Example questions

1. If 6 bolts are packed in a box, how many bolts are there in 9 boxes?

A) 45   B) 47   C) 49   D) 52   E) 54

2. If a person drinks 2 litres of water a day, how much will 3 people drink in 4 days?

A) 6 litres   B) 12 litres   C) 18 litres   D) 24 litres   E) 28 litres

1.   A. ☐   B. ☐   C. ☐   D. ☐   E. ☐

2.   A. ☐   B. ☐   C. ☐   D. ☐   E. ☐

With thanks to Perception Business Psychologists

Numerical test 3

Instructions

This exercise is similar to the previous one. There are a number of problems involving numbers and five possible answers. One and only one of the answers is correct. You have to decide which of the answers is correct, then place an X in the appropriate box.

You will not need to use a calculator for this test but you can use the pencil and paper for any rough work.

A ship is sailing to port which is 4 miles due west of its current position. Due to the wind and tide the ship is blown off course so that it is actually sailing south west. It sails south west for 5 miles before sailing 3 miles north to port.

What is the total distance travelled by the ship?

4 Miles ☐ 5 Miles ☐ 8 Miles ☐ 12 Miles ☐ 15 Miles ☐

What will be the total additional distance (in miles) travelled by the ship?

1 Mile ☐ 2 Miles ☐ 3 Miles ☐ 4 Miles ☐ 5 Miles ☐

TASK

Check your answers now against the answers at the back of the book. You can then look again at the ones you got wrong.

With thanks to Perception Business Psychologists

I've concentrated on the most popular tests for professional and managerial people. You might face a numerical speed test, so I've included some details below. Although mainly used for admin and clerical jobs, these could also be used in graduate or management selection.

Numerical speed tests

Number series/sequences

In these sorts of tests you have to fit in the gap and there is a choice of options.

For example, fill in the blank:

2, 4, 6, _, 16

There are usually patterns in these sequences which you need to spot.

In this example the answer is the sum of the previous two numbers, so the missing answer is 10 (2+4 = 6; 4+6 = 10; 6+10 = 16).

Other sequences can include numbers being squared each time, e.g. 3, 9, 81 or alternative number streams – so you could get a sequence of 2, 4, 8, 16, 32 (doubling up) and also 3, 5, 7, 9, 11 (2 added per number). When these are put together it makes finding the missing items more complex, e.g. 2, 3, 4, 5, 8, __, 16, 9, __ , 11.

Alphabet sequences

These are similar but letters of the alphabet are used instead of numbers, so A = 1, B = 2, etc.

If you do face one of these tests it is worth taking the time to list the alphabet with numbers underneath so you can use this for reference:

A	B	C	D	E	F	G	H	I	J	K	L	etc.
1	2	3	4	5	6	7	8	9	10	11	12	

Mental arithmetic questions

These involve basic numerical calculations but need to be done at speed. For example:

137 - 229

462 + 131

45 ÷ 9

27 x 6

15% of £300

Most of us would use a calculator, but obviously you have to do mental arithmetic for these. Each question would give you 4 options to choose from. Note that the answer to the first example is a minus number.

Example

How much would it cost to buy seven loaves of bread at 89p a loaf?

A. £6.23

B. £6.09

C. £6.13

D. £6.33

E. £6.43

Key tips

- The best preparation you can do is to be familiar with percentages and to get used to looking at charts, dealing with ratios and making decisions quickly.

- You will have to make calculations; it is not just looking at a chart and picking out the right answer, you also need to be able to combine different data.

- Some tests will require you to undertake some mental arithmetic so it is worth practising this as well.

- You need to keep a cool head. If you don't like numbers and maths, then reminding yourself how poor you are at these tasks will not help. That's why practice and preparation help. If you get used to working out percentages, both using a calculator and without, it will be one less thing to worry about.

- There are many more tests that you can complete via online sites; see the section at the end of Chapter 3. You can also find all of these available at:
  www.amazingpeople.co.uk/shortlisted.html.

Answers

Answers and explanations to the motoring organisations practice questions

Q2. The correct answer is B – £54. To get the answer you first have to find the cost of Bronze cover with Green Arrow from the table. The table shows you this is £30. The cost of covering two cars would therefore be £60 (2 x £30), but the question also tells you that there is a 10% discount if you take out cover for more than one car. To get the final cost, you need to find the discount (10% of £60), and subtract this from the total cost. To get 10% of £60, you need to divide £60 by 100 to get £0.6, and then multiply it by 10 to get 10% (£6). The total cost is therefore £60 - £6, which gives the answer £54.

Q3. The correct answer is B – 2:3. To get the answer you need to find the highest number that will divide into the cost of Green Arrow Silver cover (£60) and Green Arrow Gold cover (£90). The highest number is 30, which divides into the cost of Silver cover twice (60/30=2) and the cost of Gold cover three times (90/30=3). This gives you the ratio of 2:3.

Q4. The correct answer is C – 25%. To find the percentage increase you first have to find the actual increase in cost. The table tells you that the cost of Blue Star Bronze cover was £40. The question tells you this has increased to £50, giving an increase of £10.

You then have to find what percentage of the original cost (£40) the increase is (£10), by dividing the increase by the original cost. £10 divided by £40 gives you 0.25. To turn this into a percentage, multiply the answer (0.25) by 100. This gives the answer of 25%.

Chapter 6. Abstract reasoning and other tests

The previous two chapters have concentrated on verbal and numerical tests but there are other tests that you might be asked to do. This chapter covers:

- Business-learning exercises

- Abstract reasoning tests

- Diagrammatic reasoning tests

- Mechanical reasoning tests

- Checking tests

- Proof reading tests

Business-learning exercises

These are psychometric tests that are very focused on a specific job so that the company can assess if you have the aptitude to do well in this particular work area. It can also be a useful preview for you as a candidate, as if you don't like the test you will probably not be that interested in the job. The testing companies that set these tests want to see how quickly you can do something when you don't have prior knowledge, so no practice material is available.

If you are seeking work in the banking or financial sector then there might be a specific test such as one of financial appraisal where the focus is more on how quickly you can assimilate new data and draw accurate conclusions. It is worth taking the time to be clear on what needs to be done rather than to rush, as you **must** be accurate. There is often a comprehensive amount of data so read it all carefully. Whilst finance is not my favourite topic, I think the test is interesting. In one business learning exercise you are a venture capitalist and have to decide if you should invest money in a company, so think of yourself as one of the dragon's from *Dragons' Den*.

Sometimes people take these tests to see if they have the potential to move into a new area of work. I used these when a large company was going through a substantial organisational change and a financial appraisal test helped to see whether people could move into a more finance-orientated role, with other tests to check suitability for retraining as a computer programmer, systems analyst, etc. (See the end of Chapter 3 for details of a computer programmer test.)

A similar style of test can be used for people working in customer service jobs. There is one particular assessment where you have to imagine yourself working in such a role and then make decisions which have a numerical assessment involved.

Abstract reasoning tests

You can't get much more abstract than the Raven's Progressive Matrices assessment. It's the one most like an IQ test, where you get a series of shapes or symbols and have to choose the one that follows the sequence or fits in the gap from six to eight options. It's a good way to assess underlying logical reasoning aptitude, using images and diagrams rather than words.

You are less able to draw on previous experience for these sorts of tests, and some of them don't even have written instructions. Of all the tests this is the one that is most likely to assess intellect.

I've used the Raven's Progressive Matrices when working overseas with candidates applying for jobs with UK companies, as there aren't any language difficulties. There is a more advanced version – the Plus – which is used on professional and managerial people. It's generally timed and candidates have 40 minutes to complete it. A similar test is the SHL Inductive Reasoning Test.

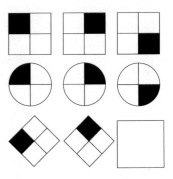

What do you think is the correct answer from the example below?

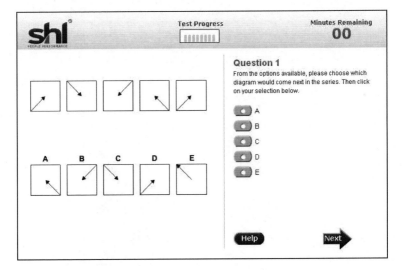

With thanks to SHL Group Ltd

The answer to this question is C. If you follow the position of the arrows you can see that it moves along, one corner at a time. So the next in the series would be for the arrow to be in the top left-hand corner.

Let's have a look at a typical instruction page, so you can see the sort of information you will get.

Abstract reasoning

The abstract reasoning test looks at your ability to identify relationships between shapes. This ability is related to testing out new ideas and solving problems.

You will see two sets of shapes, 'Set A' and 'Set B'. All of the shapes in Set A are similar in some way, and all the shapes in Set B are similar in some way. Set A and Set B are not related to each other. You have to work out how the shapes in Set A are related to each other and how the shapes in Set B are related to each other. You then have to work out whether further shapes belong to Set A, Set B or neither set.

Have a look at the practice question below. The answer to the first shape is given. Try and work out the answers to the other four shapes, and then check your answers against the explanations at the end of this chapter.

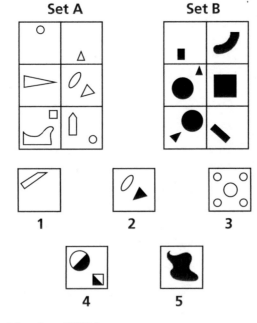

The only common feature between the cells in Set A, is that they all contain white shapes. As some of the cells in Set A contain one shape, and others contain two shapes, the number of shapes in each cell does not matter.

Similarly for Set B, all the cells contain black shapes. Again, as some cells contain one shape and others contain two, the number of shapes in each cell does not matter.

The correct answer for shape 1 is Set A, as it contains a white shape.

Now looks at 3 further examples. Work through these tests and then check your answers at the end of the book

Abstract reasoning test 1

1. Basic level

Which figure completes the series?

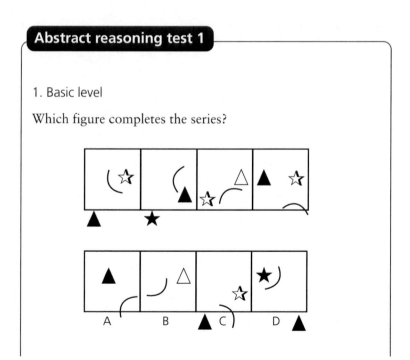

Abstract reasoning test 2

2. Intermediate level

Which figure belongs in neither group?

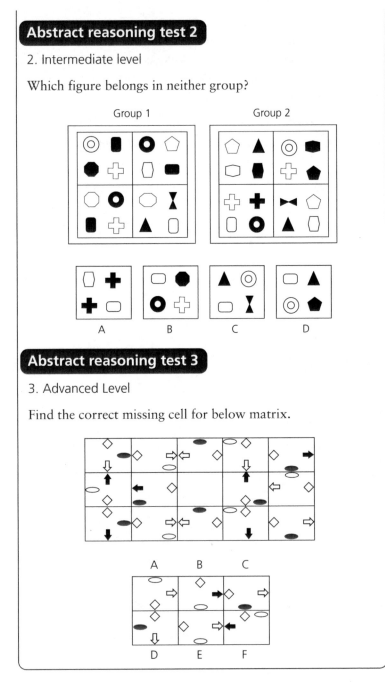

Abstract reasoning test 3

3. Advanced Level

Find the correct missing cell for below matrix.

Checking test

This sort of test is designed to assess how well you are able to spot errors that have occurred in information. You need to accurately review the material and spot any mistakes, so both speed and accuracy are both important for this sort of test.

You often get something like two lists of names and addresses and you have to check if they are the same or different. For example:

	Simon Tatler
	35b Orchard Terrace
	Halifax
	HX2 6JY
	01768 567453

Can you spot the errors (hint: there are four)?

With thanks to Perception Business Psychologists

Classification test

If you are applying for a job which requires you to sort information you may be asked to take a test which asks you to classify information into different categories according to a set of rules.

Proof reading

In this test you would get a few paragraphs of information and would need to identify any errors.

Answers

Answers and explanations to the black and white shapes practice questions

Q2. The correct answer is **Neither.** As it contains one white and one black shape, it does not clearly belong to either set.

Q3. The correct answer is **Set A,** as it contains white shapes. Although shape 3 contains five white shapes, more than any cells in Set A, it still conforms to the rules of Set A as the number of shapes is not part of the solution.

Q4. The correct answer is **Neither.** As the shapes have both black and white parts to them, they do not clearly belong to either set.

Q5. The correct answer is **Set B,** as this contains a black shape.

Chapter 7. Personality questionnaires

The previous chapters have discussed timed ability tests, but this chapter focuses on the personality questionnaire that is regularly included as part of an assessment centre. The key difference is that ability tests result in right and wrong answers, whilst personality questionnaires are looking at personality traits, such as being sociable, friendly, self-reliant or reserved. With these traits there are no right or wrong answers.

I did my first psychometric feedback session back in 1987 and I've done literally thousands since, so let me talk you through how to perform at your best.

Measuring personality is not a recent phenomenon. Over the centuries the four humours have been commonly used to describe the key different personality types.

1. **Sanguine** – someone who is light-hearted and confident, but also arrogant and likely to act on whims.

2. **Choleric** – someone who has ambition, energy and gets things done, but can also be dominant and bad tempered.

3. **Melancholic** – someone who is thoughtful and considerate but who can also be a perfectionist and become depressed.

4. **Phlegmatic** – someone who is consistent and relaxed but who may be shy and resistant to change.

These characteristics are still covered in modern-day personality questionnaires, but under different names.

Why do companies use personality questionnaires?

Companies want to find out more about candidates, especially what it is that makes them tick. Understanding more about someone's personality is helpful when considering how a person is likely to behave in different circumstances. We could of course sit down and ask people how they would behave, but a lot of people haven't given this subject any thought and so the results from the questionnaire help to structure a discussion. Also, because this is a psychometric test the results can be compared to other people, allowing us to see if someone is more or less assertive, for example, than the comparison group.

 No one passes or fails an assessment centre on the results of their personality questionnaire, but the results are used to support evidence from other assessment centre exercises.

Is there an ideal type of personality to have?

There is no such thing as a good and bad personality; we are all different and have our own strengths and weaknesses. What might be a strength in one situation or job could be a weakness in another. For example, being very conscientious is perfect in some situations but not in all. The typical advice is to just be yourself, but as I'll explain soon, you can prepare and you can make sure that you are presenting the more positive 'work' version of you.

How are personality questionnaires constructed?

Personality questionnaires are made up of a number of questions and take an average of 30-45 minutes to complete. There are some highly reputable tests which are well constructed and have a wealth of supporting data to support the validity and reliability of the test. These include (but are certainly not limited to) the 16PF5, OPQ, and Saville Consulting's Wave. There are others available that look good but which lack any research data. There are also personality questionnaires that should not be used for recruitment. The Myers-Briggs Type Indicator (MBTI) is one of the most well-known ways of identifying personality, but this is used for development and it should *never* be used for recruitment. In the time I spent writing this book two companies approached me to use the MBTI on a recruitment assignment for them. Each time I've declined, as it is unethical.

Psychometricians develop questions, check that they are valid and reliable and then present the questions to candidates, generally using a five or six point scale so you can indicate the degree to which you agree or disagree with a statement.

Examples

'I enjoy public speaking'

A	B	C	D	E
Strongly disagree	Disagree	Neutral	Agree	Strongly agree

'I try to include other people in my plans'

Never (1) Rarely (2) Occasionally (3) Sometimes (4) Often (5) Usually (6)

Some other personality questionnaires will ask you to rate which out of four or six items you like most and least. This forced choice can be quite tiresome to complete as they are usually constructed in such a way that you either like all of the options or none of them, but they do ensure you discriminate between alternatives.

The best way to prepare – understand your own personality at work

A company is interested in the 'you at work', not the 'you out of work', and plenty of us demonstrate different aspects of our personality in different situations. This can include people who are very well organised and meet deadlines at work, even if friends consider them to be much more laid back in their non-work lives.

Knowing yourself means that you can explain yourself in the follow-up interview. So if you know that you find it hard to work in an unstructured environment you can discuss how you handle this when necessary and give relevant examples.

TASK

One of the best ways of preparing for a personality questionnaire is to take some time to understand who you are, and that's what you are now going to do.

I've listed a number of areas covered by personality questionnaires and I'd like you to **think about how you would answer these**. It's worth taking the time to **note your answers**, as you can then compare these to answers from someone who knows you well. Ask them to rate you so that you can see to what extent other people share your opinion.

Understanding yourself and your personality means you will have some specific examples to show why your style is a good approach for you. People are different and we certainly don't need to approach a situation in the same way as someone else. Your preparation should include having examples ready to back up why your approach works and answering these questions is going to help.

Interpersonal style

Relating to others

1. Are you warm and friendly with people or more distant? How does that help and how does that hinder your relationships with others?

2. How confident are you at dealing with a sensitive matter involving a work colleague? What examples could you share?

3. Are you lively and spontaneous or more serious? If more serious, how do you show your enthusiasm? If more spontaneous, are there disadvantages with this?

4. How confident are you in new situations? Think of examples that demonstrate how you deal with unfamiliar situations. When are you most ill at ease?

5. To what extent will you be open with others about personal information? When has it helped to do this? When would it have been helpful to share more?

6. Are you self-reliant or a team player? Not that it is necessarily an either/or but think of examples of working well with others. Also think of times when you have had to work alone.

7. When working with people that are very different to you, how does this affect your approach?

Persuasion and influence

8. Are you highly assertive, even forceful, or more cooperative? How does this help or hinder? How do you respond to conflict?

9. How easy is it for you to motivate others? What about when it has been difficult or challenging?

10. How confident are you in expressing your opinions? What happens if your ideas are criticised? Are you a risk-taker?

11. Are you trusting or more questioning of the motives of others? Have you ever wished you were more trusting or regretted placing your trust in others?

12. What approach do you take for persuading and influencing others? How comfortable are you with this?

Thinking style

Analytical thinking

1. How do you make decisions – on the basis of a logical analysis of facts, or based on feelings and values? When does the approach work for you? Have you ever considered a different approach?

2. Are you a detail or a big-picture person? What are the benefits of your preferred approach? When would it be useful to take an alternative approach?

3. To what extent are you open to change and willing to try out new things? When would you be happier to stick with the tried and tested?

4. To what extent do you prefer to develop new ideas or to focus on practicalities, and why?

Flexibility and task focus

5. To what extent do you like structure in your work? How do you respond when there is too little or too much structure?

6. Would you consider yourself to be impulsive? Do you have control over this?

7. To what extent do you need variety and flexibility in your life and your work?

8. When a task needs to be completed, do you get it done in advance or wait till the last minute? How do you organise your work? How do you respond to the unexpected?

9. Have you ever taken control of a task? Why did you do so and what was the outcome?

10. To what extent will you follow rules? When would you be more likely to challenge rules and established ways of working?

Emotional style

1. Do you see yourself as relaxed and patient? The opposite is usually someone who may be tense and impatient but is also highly driven and energetic.

2. Think about setbacks you have experienced in life and how you have responded, was your approach effective?

3. Think about your levels of self-confidence – are you self-assured or is anything making you feel less confident?

4. Can you give an example of your drive and determination to achieve a task?

Questions related to stress

If you are feeling stressed, perhaps due to personal circumstances or because you have lost your job and are desperate for a new one, then it might show up in the test. The personality questionnaire could pose statements such as:

'I sometimes feel anxious even if things are going well.'

'I rarely worry about anything.'

Choosing between these sorts of options is seemingly straightforward, so you could decide to answer each one as if you are never stressed about anything. But a degree of tension leads to people demonstrating drive and energy; and if you always go for the 'positive' one, you may end up coming across as so laid back you are horizontal. That's the problem with trying to fake a result. Also, as a lot of companies are relating the results to competences, this part of the questionnaire may not be used in the overall decision-making process. Better to be more open and ready to discuss it in the feedback session.

Did you complete the exercise? It really is one of the best things you can do for preparation. If not go back and do it now, and don't forget to discuss this with others.

How to take a questionnaire

Personality questionnaires are often taken in advance of an assessment centre, thus allowing a report to be prepared before your one-to-one feedback session. In this case you would be sent instructions and a web link so you could take the assessment online.

On other occasions you will take the test at the assessment centre, either on a computer or using a booklet and answer sheet. Whichever method is used there will be comprehensive instructions explaining what to do, including some example questions for you to work through.

A personality questionnaire is not timed but if you do this as part of a group you will be expected to complete within a set time limit or else it will throw the timetable. The test administrator will probably walk around the room and ask you to speed up if you are slower than the other candidates, but should be subtle in the way they do this.

The instructions

Many personality questionnaires are completed online, but the instructions are similar to those if you are using a booklet and answer sheet, so the following should be helpful. Here is a typical instruction page, so you can see the sort of information you will get:

CAL: Personality Questionnaire Instructions

This CAL personality questionnaire has been designed to describe your personality in a work situation. It is not a test and there are no right or wrong answers. You are asked to rate yourself on each of the statements by choosing the rating which most applies to you.

On the answer sheet you must:

- Fill in circle A if you **strongly disagree** with the statement

- Fill in circle B if you **disagree** with the statement

- Fill in circle C if you **neither agree nor disagree** with the statement

- Fill in circle D if you **agree** with the statement

- Fill in circle E if you **strongly agree** with the statement

These ratings appear on each page of the questionnaire booklet:

A	B	C	D	E
Strongly disagree	Disagree	In-between	Agree	Strongly agree

1.	I rarely have imaginative ideas	(A)	(B)	(C)	(D)	●
2.	I enjoy speaking in public	(A)	●	(C)	(D)	(E)

In the examples above, the person has indicated that they strongly agree that the statement 'I rarely have imaginative ideas' applies to them, but they disagree that the statement 'I enjoy speaking in public' applies to them.

When completing the questionnaire you should note the following points:

- There are no right or wrong answers.

- Be honest. The information you provide may be cross-checked with other parts of the assessment process.

- Rate yourself as you really are, not how you would like to be.

- Try to avoid giving the 'C' rating as much as possible.

- Use the whole of the five point rating scale (including the extremes).

- Fully rub out any rating you wish to change.

- There is no time limit, but work as quickly as you can.

- Make sure you complete all the questions in the questionnaire.

With thanks to Criterion Partnership Ltd

Completing the test

Be truthful! It is best to go for the first answer that you think of rather than wondering about how the recruiter wants you to answer. If you try and portray a particular type of person that is different to who you are you may end up with a job that doesn't suit you, but most likely you will be found out in the discussion as there are certain questions designed to identify those people who have taken an overly positive view of themselves.

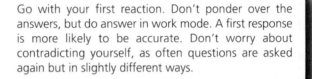

Go with your first reaction. Don't ponder over the answers, but do answer in work mode. A first response is more likely to be accurate. Don't worry about contradicting yourself, as often questions are asked again but in slightly different ways.

Certainly you want to be yourself. If you try and be somebody else you are likely to trip yourself up, but it should be you on a really good day, not the slightly neurotic you on a bad day. Nor do you want to try and portray yourself as a top sales person who is brilliant at persuading others (if you are not) as this is unlikely to match with how you present yourself in a group discussion or other assessment centre exercise.

Think of the best version of you when you complete the personality assessment, but be wary if some aspects of your personality can be seen as extreme.

Candidates will often be anxious; they want to make a good impression and to portray themselves in a positive light. So there is a tendency to try to give the answer they think the company want;

but this is hard to get right, and if you aren't careful you end up with a very skewed profile (the chart that displays the results).

For example, somebody may answer questions in such a way that they come across as someone who is very trusting and accepting of other people, rather than being more sceptical and wary of others. The first scenario is not necessarily better or worse than the second. It can depend on the work they have done, the job they are applying for and how helpful or not this approach has been to them, hence the need for a feedback discussion.

You want to be accurate and to paint a true picture of what you are like as the assessors will not be looking at the results from the personality questionnaire in isolation but alongside how you perform in the other assessment centre exercises. You don't want to lie, otherwise you are likely to trap yourself. There's no point thinking of yourself as someone with high-level negotiation skills if you fail to demonstrate this in the role-play exercise, or to see yourself as a brilliant leader if you don't have the examples to back you up at interview.

There are no right or wrong answers

Like other psychologists and test administrators I'll tell people that there are no right or wrong answers, but to some extent this is not strictly true. Of course there is no right or wrong answer to the different questions, but put together as a whole, once we look at the results there are clearly some preferable personality characteristics to have for particular jobs.

When recruiting for a sales executive I'd expect candidates to display social confidence and persuasiveness, and the results from the personality questionnaire will be used to confirm (or not) evidence from other exercises at the assessment centre. For a chief executive they need to be visionary and strategic. I want my accountant to have a high attention to detail. The assessment centre will have been well designed to gain evidence on how well the candidate matches up. So as part of your preparation you will have sought out the examples you need to demonstrate that you have the personal qualities, experience and abilities. You will want to ensure that your personality questionnaire is a good match to this.

Social desirability and honesty scales

Within a personality questionnaire there are a number of questions to assess levels of social desirability. These include questions relating to personal characteristics that most people would not want to admit to, but the way they are written means that most of us do display them occasionally. Things like:

- 'I <u>never</u> talk about people behind their back.'

- 'I have <u>never</u> failed to complete my work on time.'

Well, most of us try not to, but it is unusual for anyone *never* to do so. So this would be one of the trigger questions. Answer strongly agree to this and it triggers one of the 'social desirability scales'. The use of the word 'never' means you shouldn't agree strongly with these questions.

Honesty scales are sometimes included and include questions such as, 'If I am given too much change at a bank I would tell the bank clerk'. With these sorts of questions there should be no fudging, you should always say you would give the money back.

Critics of personality questionnaires will say that the answers to many questions are 'it depends' and of course it does. With a question such as, 'I am never distracted from a job once I have started it' could any of us say never? There will always be an occasion when you can be distracted, but think about the tasks you do; to what extent are you able to focus? I'm noted as someone who gets lots done, but as I'm writing this chapter (actually the whole book) I've been terribly distracted. I went onto Facebook to read what friends were saying, looked up music to buy on Amazon, etc, but then I focussed back on my task. I don't get so distracted that I leave a task, do something else and forget to come back to it. This is why a five or six point scale helps you to answer the questions more accurately.

Another statement: 'I believe that others find me a good listener.' Someone may believe this but the people who know them may disagree. As a psychologist I'd be talking you through this and getting examples to back up what you say. In this case, in the feedback discussion I'd ask you to give me a particular example, and then to tell me why you think that other people find you a good listener.

How long is it? How long will it take to complete?

Questionnaires vary in length but generally you will complete them in 25-45 minutes. Some of them ask you to choose between options but usually there is a five or six point scale. For some you have to choose between the option you prefer most or least, when you don't actually agree with any, or else all options sound like they apply to you. To me the worst are when you have to use a six- point scale for a number of questions but can't use the same score more than once – if you do you keep being given the questions till you prioritise them. As far as I'm concerned, these are the worst!

End of the testing session

Once you have finished answering the questions you will move onto another exercise in the assessment centre and the psychologist will score your questionnaire, produce a report and prepare for the feedback discussion.

The feedback discussion

Introduction

This will be a one-to-one session with a chartered psychologist or trained test user. There is a structure to how these run and the first few minutes of the session should be spent putting you at ease and reminding you of the confidentiality aspect, that the results will be shared with the other assessors and, if successful, a report would go to your new line manager. The test user will also ask your permission to take notes.

You are likely to be asked if you have taken a personality assessment before, and which one. You will be told the purpose of the discussion which is: *to find out more about you and how you are likely to perform on the job.*

The feedback discussion is a two-way process, and both feedback provider and candidate have an equal involvement. It's certainly not you being told what your personality is but the sharing of a hypothesis and the asking of questions.

You should be told how much time is available. Generally this will be around an hour, and if a feedback discussion lasts less than 45 minutes I don't see how it can have been done properly!

The test user should remind you that there are no right or wrong answers. You may be shown your results in the form of a graph and should be advised that there is a degree of error. For example, with a score of 6, the degree of error would mean that there is 95% accuracy for a score of 5-7.

It's helpful for a test user to emphasise to candidates that a decision is not taken on the results of this assessment alone, but it is part of a bigger process. You should also be told what happens after the discussion.

When I introduce personality questionnaires I ask candidates to be honest as I'm interested in finding out about the sort of person they are. I also tell them there will be a feedback discussion afterwards where I will seek examples to back up what they have said.

> I always ask a candidate how they were feeling when they have completed an assessment. I once interviewed someone who came across as very agitated and stressed. It turned out his wife had texted him on his way to the assessment centre to say that she was leaving him and this obviously affected his performance on the day.

The main part of the feedback discussion

You will be asked open questions to get you talking and these should be put to you in a sensitive style, e.g. rather than 'so you don't see yourself as very assertive?' it could be 'the way you have answered the questions suggests that you don't see yourself as highly assertive. What makes you think that?' This then gives the candidate a chance to agree, or not, and provide examples to support whatever they say.

Of course the discussion may not focus purely on the results of the personality assessment. Many companies use competency frameworks so the feedback session may be structured more around the competences, with the personality questionnaire results used to support the questions asked.

Report

Some companies will give you a detailed report, others will only provide a one-page summary, but all feedback can be helpful to review later. If you are successful in your application you are likely to get a more detailed report. If not, ask!

You should now be much clearer on what to expect. If it would help to complete a personality questionnaire the sites below should be helpful, or if you would prefer an in-depth psychometric feedback discussion please get in touch with me.

Resources

Undertake a free personality questionnaire at:

www.bbc.co.uk/science/humanbody/mind/surveys/personality/index.shtml

For a personality questionnaire based on the '5 factor' model (which underpins most personality questionnaires) you could visit

www.findingpotential.com or www.shlquestionnaires.com/1001/

where you will also get a free report.

There are plenty more available but these are two of the most reputable ones.

You can also find all of these at:
www.amazingpeople.co.uk/shortlisted.html.

Assessment Centres

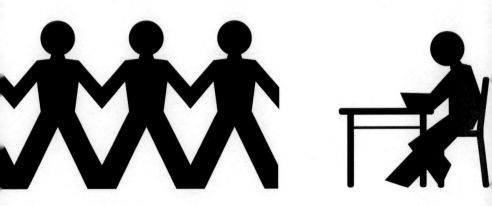

Chapter 8. Assessment centres – an introduction

An assessment centre is not a place but a combination of exercises designed to help a company make effective decisions over who gets selected for the job. From an assessor and company point of view it means there are lots of opportunities for candidates to demonstrate how they match up to the competences required for success in a job, and candidates get lots of opportunities to show their strengths.

Assessment centres go back to 1943 when they were used by the War Office Selection Board to select officers. Prior to this, decisions were made based on people's backgrounds, but many people who had potential were missed, and others that had been selected were 'returned to unit' because of lack of ability. In peacetime, assessment centres were initially used by the civil service and other parts of the public sector, and there is plenty of published evidence that assessment centres are good predictors of performance.

20 years ago candidates were doing things like building towers out of Lego and discussing non-job related topics such as prohibition of blood sports, but these sorts of activities have given way to more work-related tasks and activities.

Assessment centres comprise a number of different exercises – interview, psychometric tests of ability and personality, group discussion, presentations, etc, – with a number of assessors. Judgements are made based on the combination of information from the exercises and assessors. The overall evaluation is only made at the end.

These chapters on assessment centres cover the same ground I teach my personal clients. The only difference is that it isn't personalised to the actual assessment centre you are going to attend.

I've designed hundreds of assessment centres. With some large-scale campaigns where 20 or more people are being recruited I've had a decent budget to do things properly, and many of the assessment centres I've worked on that have been designed by others have been similarly well researched. It's not always cost-effective to do this, however, and for a one-off campaign the budget has usually been more limited, but the activities candidates have been asked to undertake have been matched with the requirements of the job.

Not all companies will use assessment centres. They are more common in larger companies (most well-known organisations utilise them) and in the public service, particularly the civil service and police force. They are more likely to be used for graduate and professional jobs, where the investment in the costs of design and assessment are worthwhile. Other companies will use elements of assessment centres and frequently people are asked to make a presentation, followed by questions, in addition to an interview. This is not a 'proper' assessment centre, but the advice in the subsequent chapters will be very useful to you.

I'm going to be talking about competences quite a lot and I don't want you to be unclear, so here's a simple definition:

Competences are the clusters of knowledge, skills and other attributes that describe effective performance for a given role. They are used by almost all major companies including the civil service, Royal Mail, Goldman Sachs, Vodafone, etc. Typical competences include strategic thinking, commercial awareness and interpersonal sensitivity.

People often become very apprehensive about assessment centres, they see the number of activities they are to perform and worry about what to do. This section will help to take away the fear and you will probably look back on the day and realise you enjoyed it. A key benefit is that it gives you lots of opportunities to demonstrate your strengths and to shine.

How an assessment centre is created

Let's assume there is a reasonable budget and I'll talk you through the steps assessment centre designers go through. By reading about the process it helps remove the mystique and lets you know what to expect.

Step 1: Find out about the job and ideal candidate

Which job is being recruited for? What information is already available? Is a job description or person specification available and is this still appropriate for the job? I often talk to people who have a significant stake in the particular job – manager, peers, internal customers, and occasionally external customers – to find out more about the job and the key characteristics they're looking for.

Step 2: Identify the competences needed to perform well in the job

Companies often have company-wide competences, but the specific indicators will vary depending on the level of the job. Some companies have far too many so I need to help identify the top six or so and rank them if appropriate. Some of the companies I've consulted with want candidates to be assessed on 9-12 competences, but this is far too many for assessors to deal with.

Step 3: Choose the exercises

Once we know the competences there's a need to choose exercises that are going to be used to measure these competences. Each competency has to be measured at least twice, with no more than five competences in any one exercise. Some of the competences could be measured in almost every exercise, and for some it may be a struggle to measure them more than once. That's where the skill of an experienced psychologist comes in, as they can create an exercise to capture relevant evidence from the candidates.

Exercises can fall into a number of categories:

- **Group exercises:** Predominately a group discussion but also team-based activities, sometimes aimed at assessing leadership ability.

- **Written exercises:** For example, case studies, e-tray (in-tray) exercises, strategy papers, etc.

- **Exercises involving the assessor or actors:** Presentations and role-plays often involving customers plus the interviewer!

- **Psychometrics:** Personality questionnaires and ability tests.

A typical assessment centre will start with ability testing, it will then move onto a group exercise and then have activities happening in parallel, so each candidate takes the same exercises but in a different order.

In the timetable you can see that following the group activities there are four options which are carried out at different times for each candidate. These are:

1. Customer meeting

2. Presentation

3. Role-play

4. Personality feedback discussion

	Candidate 1	Candidate 2	Candidate 3	Candidate 4
08.30	Introductions			
08.45	Group discussion			
09.30	Psychometrics			
10.30	Role-play	Presentation	Psychometric feedback	Customer meeting
11.45	Customer meeting	Role-play	Presentation	Psychometric feedback
13.00	Lunch			
13.45	Psychometric feedback	Customer meeting	Role-play	Presentation
15.00	Presentation	Psychometric feedback	Customer meeting	Role-play
16.15	Concluding session, including what happens next			
16.45	Assessors' discussion and decision making			

When designing an assessment centre, other questions need to be addressed:

- **Will the exercises be seen as relevant?** Deciding to use a particular exercise is not enough. The exercise has to be relevant to the job being assessed and also for the level of the job. If it isn't it lacks 'face validity' with the candidates and they may not want to be active participants.

- **Will the exercise assess what it needs to?** As a psychologist I also need to make sure that it will assess the relevant competences. For example, if a group exercise should be measuring 'strategic thinking' and 'influence' then the materials provided and the way the exercise is introduced should make this possible.

- **Will one candidate be favoured over the rest?** We also need to make sure that we don't overly favour one particular candidate. For example, if there are both internal and external candidates the exercises can't be written in a way that expects particular company knowledge that would not be available to the external candidates.

- **Will the assessors be able to accurately assess the exercises?** Assessors are trained but many only assess a few times a year. Accordingly, the exercises need to be designed so that the assessors can mark each exercise accurately, and there needs to be consistency between all assessors.

Step 4: Choose the assessors

An assessment centre will comprise a team of assessors, including line managers, HR and external consultants (often chartered psychologists). The use of external consultants helps bring a wider, non-corporate perspective and because they are highly experienced they should be accurate in their assessment decisions. Line managers give credibility, and candidates like to be interviewed by the people they will work for and with. They are also able to answer many more of the company specific questions that can be asked.

The assessors should be experienced in this field. Many will have gone through a three or five day training programme where they have learnt about different exercises, how all the exercises are put together and have been taught about the role of psychometrics. For each new exercise the assessors should get a chance to read it through in advance and also to have completed it themselves, enabling them to see what they would be able to do under time constraints.

Step 5: Prepare the exercises

This is where both research and creative skill comes into play. Sometimes exercises can be taken 'off the shelf' but often it is necessary to develop something specific for the job. This is usually based on the job description and the tasks the successful candidate may need to undertake. For example, produce a presentation outlining the most important issues to be tackled in the first six months in the job, or dealing with a role-play client meeting typical of the work the job involves. For the designer it is not just a case of developing an exercise but also working out a scoring framework, i.e. what sort of responses will score high, mid range and low points, with guidance for the assessors.

Step 6: Trial the exercises

It's not always cost-effective to do a trial, but if this is a large-scale recruitment scheme, such as for graduate trainees, it is essential to make sure the exercises work. For a more bespoke recruitment exercise, such as when recruiting a new finance director, it may not be cost-effective to do so, in which case careful attention needs to be paid to ensure the exercises are both relevant and measure essential criteria for the job.

Step 7: Send out information to candidates

When you are invited to an assessment centre you should be provided with some detail. Whilst some companies will give you a full timetable for the day, others are more vague. You may only get instructions on where to meet and may not even know whether it is going to be a very full day or just a morning. This has happened a couple of times to my clients in recent months. They assumed they were going for a full-day assessment centre when it was actually just an interview and presentation so it only took half a day. It's always worth phoning up to see what else you can find out.

I really don't understand why some companies are so secretive about the content of the day; I always assume this is just because everything is being prepared at the last minute, so they don't know either!

Step 8: Running the assessment centre

The people you will meet at the assessment centre will be the assessors, the centre manager and possibly a test administrator. The centre manager should greet you when you arrive, make you feel welcome and talk you through what will happen during the day.

Usually you have a timetable that tells you what you will be doing and when (see earlier example), but occasionally you get a different sort of timetable. I've attended an assessment centre that included preparing for a presentation, analysing a case study, and an interview, and I was responsible for my time during the day. I was to be taken for an interview and to make my presentation but I didn't know when. I assume the timetable was done this way to see how I would manage my day, but it is quite a stressful approach. I hope you don't face something similar but if you do then planning is essential. I suggest that you list the tasks and estimate how long each one will take. If you are required to make a presentation then this has to take priority, but don't spend so long on this element that you fail to complete all the exercises.

ORCE – Observe, Record, Classify, Evaluate

During the assessment centre the assessors will **observe** your behaviour and **record** (take notes) on what you say and do. Only at the end of the exercise will they **classify** the evidence against the different competences being assessed and finally they **evaluate** to a standard.

A typical day at an assessment centre

Different companies run assessment centres in different ways. They usually only last a day, which means you only need to take one day off work, but there will be an early start.

- Arrive by 8.30 am and be met by an administrator who will check your personal details
- Meet fellow candidates and be talked through how the day will go
- Preparation for the first exercise, which is usually a group discussion
- Meet the assessors who introduce themselves just before the group discussion starts
- Time for a short break before undertaking a timed ability test (this double checks results if a test was undertaken at home)
- Have a discussion with a psychologist about the results from the psychometric assessments
- Prepare for role-play exercise and then have the practical assessment
- Lunch
- Prepare for a meeting with a 'customer' and then have the practical assessment
- Present your review presentation (prepared in advance) to an assessor
- Meet with assessment centre manager to be told what happens next

Throughout there will be some free time. You may be happy to chat with your fellow candidates, particularly if this is for graduate recruitment where a number of jobs are to be filled, but if the other candidates are competitors you may prefer to take some time to yourself, perhaps to go for a short walk or to read something you have brought along.

There is some follow up action you can take, which might make a difference, so do read Chapter 20 after your interview or assessment centre.

Step 9: Assessors classify and evaluate the evidence

At the end of each exercise the assessors will rate your performance. They will read the detailed description of each competence and gather together relevant examples (evidence), both positive and negative.

They will then use the scoring key to give you an overall rating against each competence in the exercise being assessed. This can be a four, five or six point scale. For example:

Excellent (Showed multiple clear evidence of a high level of competence with no substantial negative evidence)	6
Good (Showed clear evidence of competence and little negative evidence)	5
Acceptable (Showed more positive evidence than negative evidence)	4
Not acceptable (Showed sufficient negative evidence to be judged lacking in competence)	3
Weak (Showed more negative evidence than positive evidence)	2
Poor (Showed multiple clear evidence of a lack of competence with no substantial positive evidence)	1

Step 10: Making a decision

After the assessment centre exercises are completed the centre manager will do a final session thanking all the candidates for their participation and telling them what will happen next.

The assessors then meet and discuss the results from each exercise, bringing together the results to build an overall picture of the candidates. This is called the integration or 'wash up' session. Each candidate is usually discussed in turn. Firstly, the results from the psychometric tests are shared, including a review from the personality questionnaire. Then each exercise is discussed in turn – so each of the assessors discuss the exercise they observed and provide a score. Then the assessors can step back and consider the overall results – has this particular candidate met the standard, are there any concerns, etc?

Once all candidates have been discussed, the final decision is reached. Perhaps none of the candidates are good enough and so the company need to advertise again. Or perhaps there are two excellent candidates and just one job, so the choice may be difficult. Sometimes the final candidates are seen by a key representative from the company, particularly when an independent consultancy company have run the assessment centre.

Step 11: Review the process and give feedback to unsuccessful candidates

Once a decision has been reached, the whole process should be reviewed; what went well and should be repeated, was anything unclear and needs improving? Time should also be set aside to consider the assessors; being candid, were they all up to the job? Some assessors can be slow but thorough, but if they hold up the rest of the exercises then it does not make for an effective team. Others may have been weak in their classification of the evidence and thus may need further training.

The lessons for you

At an assessment centre it is hard to perform above your capability but easy to perform below it, so stay focused.

Treat every exercise independently, and don't let your concern that you have done poorly on one exercise affect the next one. Do something to distract yourself, such as sitting in your car and blasting out some upbeat music for a few minutes or writing your shopping list.

I once interviewed somebody who spent over 10 minutes telling me how badly they had done in their presentation. Some of the answers they gave to my questions were then very vague. I definitely think that wondering how they had done and going over everything they thought had gone wrong was not good for their performance. Most of us are quite bad at predicting how well, or not, we have done. In this person's case the presentation had gone fine and he had reached an acceptable standard; alas he didn't do so well with me, and didn't get offered a job.

Dinner with assessors and candidates

You may be invited to a dinner on the night before the assessment centre, or your assessment centre may last for two days and at a residential centre you will have dinner with candidates and assessors. This is **not** the time to let your hair down and have a few too many beers. By all means have a drink or two, but keep your wits about you. Do not think the assessors are off duty, whatever they say. Even if not formally assessing, they will notice your level of social competence.

Some companies will sit the candidates with the assessment centre manager and the assessors on another table. This is probably the best way to run an assessment centre as it does mean that there is a clear divide between assessed and non-assessed time. However, other companies will sit everybody together for dinner. You will need to be able to chat to the other people on the table and sometimes current affairs will be discussed so make sure you are up-to-date with the news. If people are sat at a long table it is less easy for them to talk and sometimes assessors will swap seats between courses.

As a psychologist I've been asked to give my opinion of each candidate based on their behaviour at the dinner. In one memorable event with a very assertive chief executive he frowned on any candidate who skipped the gin and tonic and wine, as socialising was an important part of the job. This particular man was also seeking an HR director who would stand up to him, so when the discussion became controversial he saw more potential in those who were assertive in their views rather than those who were merely agreeable.

> I once applied for a job with a water company and asked for mineral water as a pre-dinner drink. With hindsight that was not a good choice!

Pre-reading

Some companies will send you pre-reading in advance of the assessment centre and this should be read carefully. You don't need to do further reading on the subject but make sure you fully understand what is supplied.

To keep things fair and objective it's unlikely that you will be able to take this information into the assessment centre venue with you. That's because candidates could have prepared possible answers or annotated the material in a way that might give them an advantage. You are given a clean copy of the background reading on arrival at the assessment centre.

The pre-reading can also include details on the competences to be assessed and some companies provide a detailed explanation of these. For example, rather than just saying 'Communication' it has been expanded to include:

- Write effectively
- Speak effectively
- Actively listen
- Persuade and influence

- Represent and promote

- Customer focused

- Negotiate

- Consult and involve

You can see that this is a broad competence, covering both written and oral communication as well as listening skills and being able to persuade and negotiate. Often people do well on some but not all of the competency indicators.

For one particular job with the civil service, shortlisted candidates are sent comprehensive background materials that are referred to at the assessment centre. The materials include details on all the competences to be assessed and also details of the different exercises to be undertaken. For this particular assessment centre there are three separate exercises to be undertaken – an electronic e-tray exercise, a role-play with a direct report and a role-play with a peer from within the organisation.

Like many assessment centres the scenario is set in the future and is fictitious, so it means you aren't disadvantaged if you don't have any current knowledge about it, but you do need to concentrate on the material supplied. When a topic is set in the future, you also can't make assumptions, as who knows what things will be like in 10 years time.

Chapter 9. Group exercises

Most companies want employees who get on and can communicate well with each other. People can say that they can do this, but can they really prove it? That's why companies include group exercises as part of an assessment centre; they want to see how well you relate with other people. As a psychologist I know that we can't be 100% confident about how someone has performed based on just one exercise (dependent on the people and the topic we may feel much more confident in some groups than others), and ideally candidates would do two or even three exercises, but this isn't practical.

This chapter is going to talk you through the different types of group exercises you may encounter, with some general tips on how to perform at your best and specifics for each particular exercise.

A typical group exercise will be for four or six people, and they are designed to work with any number between four and six. However, due to last minute illness sometimes a group is down to three people and so the exercise is unlikely to work effectively. In such cases a 'ringer' is introduced, who is often a recent entrant but sometimes an administrator. Their involvement is quite low-key and you are often unaware that they are not a candidate until later.

Preparation

Every group exercise allows some preparation time although it might be short, with just time to read through simple instructions. Depending on the exercise you will either prepare in a separate room and then be taken to the discussion room or you will prepare in the discussion room and the assessors will come and join you. The former usually occurs in larger scale assessments such as for graduate recruitment where all candidates prepare together, supervised by a test administrator.

The amount of time you have to prepare will differ depending on the exercise. For some it will be five minutes to read through the instructions to ensure you are clear on what you need to do, for others you may get around 20 minutes when you have a significant amount of reading to do.

At this point you don't know if you all have the same or different briefs. As you read through, if it suggests a particular outcome is preferred it might be useful to think of the pros and cons.

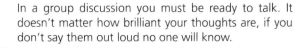

In a group discussion you must be ready to talk. It doesn't matter how brilliant your thoughts are, if you don't say them out loud no one will know.

Before the assessment centre

You could practise taking part in a group exercise with a group of family or friends – create a number of topics, ask someone to pick one at random and allow 20-30 minutes for a discussion. At the end ask everyone to give you feedback on one thing you did well, and one way to improve. This could cover body language, voice tone, clarity of comments, etc. This will not be as effective as doing one for real but can help you become more familiar with this type of exercise.

You should also think about the sort of person you are in a group. Not everybody is a good team-player, so consider how you can bring out your best when working with others. If you are quiet, what sort of questions could you ask, perhaps about the process, so that you do speak early on?

Make sure you understand **active listening skills**. You can read more about them in Chapter 2.

The assessors

Generally there will be half the number of assessors as there are candidates but sometimes you can find you have more people observing than candidates, particularly when a consultancy company are running the assessment but some of the managers from the company want to see the candidates in action. In a typical six person discussion there will be three assessors each observing two candidates each. They usually sit behind desks or have clipboards and will be taking comprehensive notes on their two candidates.

Assessors are taught to observe and record whilst an exercise is happening so don't be surprised to see them writing extensive notes. They will be making notes on what you say and how you say it, your voice tone and also any non-verbal behaviours and body language, so if you are sat back and looking disinterested this will be picked up on. They will also notice if you nod in agreement to points other people make.

Assessors read through the instructions that candidates receive and are aware of the competences being assessed so they will be gathering examples (evidence) for evaluation at a later stage.

If you haven't already met the assessors and this is the first exercise (which it often is) then they will introduce themselves by name and provide brief details on their role – operations manager, external consultant, etc.

Sometimes the administrator will remind the candidates of the instructions and say that the assessors will start the exercise once they are all seated. In this case the exercise starts very quickly. In other cases candidates will have prepared in advance but the final instructions for the exercise are provided by one assessor.

An assessor will remind the candidates of the amount of time allowed and ask the candidates to start. Often you will hear no more from them until the end.

Sometimes there may be interruptions built into the exercise to see how you as a group react to new information and sometimes there is a second part to the exercise. This takes a different approach to the discussion and will often focus on an area that was not discussed in any depth. For example, when the group had to choose between options, and one was discarded, this is the one that the group will be asked to discuss.

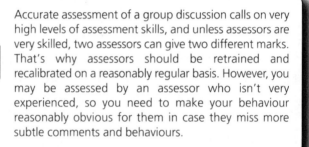

Accurate assessment of a group discussion calls on very high levels of assessment skills, and unless assessors are very skilled, two assessors can give two different marks. That's why assessors should be retrained and recalibrated on a reasonably regular basis. However, you may be assessed by an assessor who isn't very experienced, so you need to make your behaviour reasonably obvious for them in case they miss more subtle comments and behaviours.

Let's now look at the different styles of group exercise in more detail.

Group exercises

Assigned role group discussion

Some discussions will be based on you having an assigned role, and these are popular in graduate assessment centres such as the civil service Fast Stream.

Your preparation would include some general information that every candidate gets and then something specific to your role, such as representing a particular organisation or department. These discussions are often, like other test scenarios at assessment centres, set in the future, often 10 years ahead, to make sure that people are not at an advantage through using any current knowledge they may have.

The candidate briefs are carefully prepared to ensure that they are evenly weighted, although depending on your own interests you might find that you are more drawn to some briefs than others. The briefs are put together so that you have strong support for one option, you support a second, perhaps are ambivalent to a third and disagree with a fourth. Based on this, there will be an ally within the group, and it is useful to establish who this person is so that you can work together.

I've used similar styles for other positions, such as recruiting a marketing manager for a university. Each candidate was given one page of general background explaining that there are four faculties each bidding to secure funding of £50,000, which is only available to one faculty, and they had to determine which would get it. Each candidate then received their own individual brief. In this particular group exercise, 15 minutes were allocated to pre-reading and preparation, followed by a 50-minute discussion. During the preparation time candidates needed to think about an idea that would be convincing to others.

In this particular exercise candidates were told that they needed to:

- Individually generate an idea of how they would use the money
- Promote the idea to the group and persuade others that it is the best option
- Be willing to consider and evaluate each option
- Agree who gets the money (it can't be split!)

Groups will tackle these discussions in different ways, but it is helpful to agree a plan of action, to share information and for it to have some focus. There is an expectation that this will be an exchange of views and you need to support your argument with evidence from your brief, not just assertion.

Assessors like this type of group exercise, as all participants need to talk early on, which means they can't slip into a role of high/low contributor. As a group they need to problem solve and candidates also have to negotiate any conflict.

> Don't forget to keep track of time to make sure that you move beyond a sharing of information and you focus on the task you have been set.

Unassigned role group discussion

In this discussion you are not assigned roles but can take your own view on the particular subject. You will be asked to discuss information and reach a conclusion. This could be related to the job or something in the news.

Topics could include 'how to get more customers', 'how to get media coverage', or being put in a scenario set 10 or 20 years into the future where you need to think about how you would deal with a particular situation. For example, discussing ways to reduce energy usage, or a discussion on how to get more young people involved in sport. It could be something perceived as fun, such as organising a large celebration or an awards ceremony. You would have some time to prepare on your own, followed by the group discussion. Influencing and negotiating skills are often important competences and you should look to demonstrate your skills in these areas. Sometimes the discussion is based on a topical issue, so it is helpful to keep up with current affairs, or something related to the job you are applying for. As always, preparation will help.

Another popular topic is to say that the group are the trustees of a charity and as a group you need to decide which of a number of worthy causes gets the money (it can only go to one charity). You will have prepared your own case during your preparation time.

A third unassigned group task is when you work with three or five other people to address a business or personnel problem such as:

> Due to the current economic climate, one of the directors has suggested that company cars should be withdrawn from all managers who don't have an essential need for a car. It is anticipated that this would be met with resistance and some staff may decide to look for a job elsewhere. The director is aware of this but insists that if this cutback isn't made job losses are likely. What would you recommend in response to this suggestion?

As a group you then need to recommend what specific action should be taken.

You are given a group task which is a problem to be solved

This type of group exercise differs from the other two as each candidate is given some information and you need to share this in order to solve the task.

There are a number of exercises that are based on the same approach. Cards have been created which refer to a number of individuals, and, for example, the type of house they live in (e.g. a bungalow) the car they drive (e.g. a sports car), and their type of pet (e.g. a dog). You have to share the information so that as a group you can work out the answers to the question, which could be 'who lives in the town house and who owns a poodle?' All participants need to talk early on, which means they can't slip into a role of high/low contributor.

You must work together as a group and share information. I've observed this type of exercise many times and am always surprised by candidates who keep information to themselves and don't want to share. This is not a good approach as the group needs all the information to solve the problem.

This exercise is partly about memory, and if, like me, you have a poor memory it can be tough. It can help to listen carefully and repeat and summarise what has been found out. Remember the game where you go around a circle starting with A and you have to remember all the items that have gone before so by the time you are at E you are saying – I went to the shops and bought an apple, a briefcase, a computer, a dog and an emu? Well that might help, *if* you knew this sort of exercise was coming up, but you won't know so it might be wasted preparation.

You are given a practical activity (work-related)

Sometimes the assessment centre designers decide to give people a more practical-based exercise, and there are valid arguments that this works better as it is closer to 'real life'.

You would work together with your fellow candidates to do something such as producing an advert. It's often worth taking time to plan how to make use of the time at the start of the exercise and to keep track of time once you begin.

For many jobs, working as part of a team is very important and that is what the assessor will be looking for. It's hard to keep up a persona of a team player if you aren't, and those who are highly competitive at the expense of others find it hard to keep this trait in check.

You are set a scenario and you need to make a decision

This is another exercise where candidates work together as part of a team to achieve a task. In this particular exercise you are placed in an imaginary scenario and have to decide what to do.

A typical discussion would be 'desert survival'. The scenario is that you were all on a plane which has crashed and you have to individually put into order the items worth saving, including a mirror, which would help you to signal for help, and a tarpaulin, which is useful for shelter and to catch water.

Remember, if you are stranded somewhere, being detected is your priority, followed by drink and food. It's also important to stay with the vehicle if you can as search parties look for your last location. There is lots more information available on this particular exercise on the internet.

Non work-related tasks

Some companies, thankfully very few, are still using group tasks which bear little connection to a job, such as building things out of bricks, or looking to safely transport an egg, using items on the table, from one side of the table to another. Whilst these can be useful as team-building and development activities, candidates can, quite rightly, challenge the validity of such an experience as part of recruitment.

If you are quiet – roles you can play within a group

The note taker

A group usually needs someone to act as scribe. This can be an effective role, but too many people fall into the role of secretary, just noting what other people say and writing things down without any thought, so the notes are not helpful. What you have to do is be more of a facilitator, asking questions. You also need to be organised so you can structure what is said, and of course you do need to write legibly if the flip charts are to be of use.

The timekeeper

If you are going to be the timekeeper then make sure you do keep accurate time. Ideally, you would go beyond saying 'we've used 10 minutes', and make a comment that helps move the group forward.

The internal candidate exercise

If you are applying for a promotion within your current company the exercise can differ as the assessors will assume you understand your company's operation, names of departments, mission and vision, etc.

A typical exercise would be that you are all area managers within a specific region and you are to participate in a quarterly area managers' meeting. Each of you (six candidates) will have a brief containing material relevant to you all plus other information specific to you. Each candidate will have a problem to be discussed at the meeting. During the meeting each person leads a discussion of their problem, summarises and then the discussion moves on to the next person.

Here is a typical introduction to this sort of exercise:

> The exercise is in **three** parts.
>
> The first part lasts for **15 minutes** and you need to familiarise yourself with this brief.
>
> The second part lasts **one hour** and involves each of you presenting your problem to the others in the group and leading a discussion of it for 10 minutes. The regional manager, who is well-known for taking a back seat in these sorts of meetings, will chair the discussion but this will be limited to asking people in turn to lead the group and keeping people to their 10-minute time limit.
>
> The third part lasts for **15 minutes**. You will be asked to produce a report on the discussion of your problem to be sent to your assistant manager before you leave for a one-week business strategy course where you have committed to take time away from the day-to-day running of your business and so will be unavailable to answer any questions that may come up.

Example: Specific instructions for the Bristol Area Manager

You are the Bristol Area Manager.

You have fifteen minutes to read, analyse and make notes on your problem stated below, so that you are ready to brief the other managers on it and lead a discussion of it. Your problem will take up to 10 minutes of the meeting.

The problem that you face in the Bristol area is the very strong competition from Rival Co. & Son, who has opened up less than 500 yards from you. With their aggressive marketing approach and special offers this has had a noticeable impact on your monthly figures (see attached sheets). An analysis of the competitor's products and prices compared with ours is also attached.

You need to get ideas from your fellow managers for a local marketing campaign, or for some other response to the competition that is in-line with company policy.

As you can see, this group exercise then leads on to a written exercise. Assessment centres often combine exercises in this way.

Leadership exercises

For some jobs it is very important that you demonstrate your leadership abilities, e.g. if applying for a job in the armed forces, but this can also be used in other circumstances. Such qualities could be assessed by having you steer a group of people to achieve a task, varying from building a tower out of Lego to getting a group of people across a river using two oil drums, rope and a saw.

Rotating leadership exercises

In some exercises everyone takes turns to be in charge. When it's your turn, take a consultative rather than a directive approach; listen to other people and encourage contributions from others:

- Be clear on the task and what needs to be achieved.

- Recognise that others may have good ideas and be willing to build on them.

- Be clear and concise in what you have to say.

- Delegate tasks such as note taker and timekeeper.

- Don't necessarily back down when challenged.

- If there is any sign of conflict, look for ways to solve it.

- If you are outgoing be careful not to say too much and don't forget to listen.

- Don't try to win at the expense of others; put-downs are not appreciated.

- Make sure that the task is completed within the time allowed.

Commenting on other candidates

Occasionally you may be asked to comment on other candidates. This could be to rate their performance, or to decide who was the most effective against certain criteria, so do pay some attention to the others. You are not normally told that you will need to do this in advance. The first time I faced this situation I did really badly, I couldn't even remember the names of the other candidates in the discussion. From then on I made sure that I had written down details of who sat where on my personal copy of the timetable so I could use that as a prompt.

Group exercise performance review

Some companies will ask you to review your performance either by completing a questionnaire or via an interview. Following a group discussion you could be asked questions such as:

- How did you think it went?

- Did you agree with the decision made?

- How do you think you performed?

- Were you able to put across all your ideas? If not, what stopped you saying something?

- Were you able to say everything you wanted to say?

- Did you think your ideas were taken up?

- Was there anything you would have liked to say but didn't?

- If you were going to do it again, would you do anything differently?

- So be ready to comment but don't think you need to put a positive spin on everything; assessors are usually looking to make sure that your self-assessment is accurate and matches with that of the assessor.

General tips

- Have a highlighter ready as you go through the instructions to enable you to mark any key points. This makes it easier for you to remember significant points.

- Speak up. No matter how many good ideas and thoughts you have, unless you speak you won't be given any credit for them.

- Ignore the assessors, don't look at them, and concentrate on the group. They don't appreciate candidates who 'play to the gallery'.

- The longer you go without speaking, the harder it is to join in. You don't want to say something irrelevant, so commenting on the process could be helpful.

- If you notice somebody is very quiet, ask for their opinion or thoughts to bring them into the discussion.

- If someone has taken over the group and is bulldozering through the discussion ask a question to check how much support there is for this particular view.

- Don't be afraid to summarise what's been said, both at the end and part way through – assessors like this.

- If you tend to be quiet, volunteer to keep track of the time as this will give you a reason to speak up. If you do this, make sure that you do keep an accurate track of time otherwise you will be penalised by the assessors. Do give a warning to the group when there is, say, 10 minutes left.

- Being the most vocal isn't necessary the best approach. Is what you are saying relevant? Are you taking over and not giving others a chance to speak?

- Be involved and interested in what other people have to say. In addition, refer to people by name as assessors always like this. Sometimes your fellow group members will wear name badges, but if not draw a little diagram on your notepad that you can refer to.

- Lean forward into the group to show your interest in both the activity and what other people have to say.

- If you agree with a point do nod supportively.

- If you disagree, make your point constructively and make sure you avoid personal criticism or strident comments.

- One way to challenge someone is to do it through asking a question, such as 'that's an interesting point, what makes you say that?'

- If you are challenged by one of the other candidates, don't go on the defensive; it's far better to ask them to explain why they think the way they do. Make sure that you continue to contribute, otherwise if you go quiet the assessors will think that you don't respond well to criticism.

- Sometimes a white board or flip chart can be used, but check the notes as you may not be allowed to use it. By standing at the flip you may find yourself in a position where you can be actively involved by asking questions and summarising, but make sure you do get involved throughout and don't end up as a secretary.

- The actual conclusion reached is less important than the discussion (in most cases) so make sure to work well as a group but also ensure that you are moving forward and not stuck due to, perhaps, no one summarising and reminding the group of the need to achieve the task.

- Do retain a sense of humour throughout the discussion.

Chapter 10. Written exercises

Analytical skills are crucial for many jobs and companies will want to see how well you can analyse written information, particularly when you are given a comprehensive amount of information to read under time constraints. Written exercises will assess to what extent you can quickly understand sometimes complex data, how you make judgements, whether your decisions are sound and if you are demonstrating some commercial awareness.

Whilst you can tell an interviewer that you can do this and can even bring along examples of what you can do, assessors will want to see how well you can produce something under pressure.

Many of the written exercises are job-related. For example, if you were to apply for a job as the chief executive at a national charity you may have to put a report together in response to a premise such as:

> You have learned that one of the divisions of the charity is dissatisfied with the umbrella nature of the organisation and they have said that unless changes take place they will leave their membership and set up their own organisation. You need to prepare a written paper on how you will respond.

The written task

A written exercise can be standalone or could follow on from another, such as the e-tray exercise. In this case an email will ask you to reply within the next, say, 30 minutes. If it is in these circumstances, don't ignore emails you have seen and replied to as part of the earlier exercise and don't forget to review the information in the folders.

Communication paper

Some assessment centre exercises are very relevant to a job. If you were applying for a job with a PR company, key aspects of the job include:

- Writing and editing leaflets and brochures

- Producing press releases

- Writing talks and speeches

- Writing copy for newsletters and websites

Therefore writing a press release might be an element of the assessment centre. Your brief would provide you with some background information and your instructions would give you a specific amount of time to produce (in this case) a press release.

> The best preparation for a job which involves a significant writing element is to practice writing under time constraints.

Sometimes the assessor will just read and assess your paper but often this is followed by an interview where the assessor will want to ask you questions such as:

- How did you approach this task?

- How did you decide what the key messages should be, etc?

Business case study – policy exercise

A case study can be used to assess you for a number of competences, often including communication, critical thinking and analytical skills. Sometimes you will just be asked to produce a written brief but often it is followed by a presentation and question and answer section. You will often be given data on three options and need to analyse the pros and cons of each, make a recommendation and make it clear why you have chosen that particular option.

> If numerical data is included you must make use of this or you will be penalised.

Some case studies can be very comprehensive, containing numerous sheets of paper. One case study I recently assessed contained 17 separate documents, each with detailed information. In this particular type of written exercise there is an initial page of candidate instructions which sets the scene and tells you what you need to do. You get this at the start of the exercise and the administrator will check all is clear so do ask if not.

When you approach this sort of task make sure you have **read the instructions clearly** and do exactly what it says. If you need to pick out the key operational issues, than make sure that they are clearly stated. If you are asked to consider implications, then do so – looking at both positive and negative issues. It might involve taking a more strategic and commercial approach, looking beyond the specific question, particularly for senior jobs. You may be asked to evaluate something – this is not being descriptive but taking a critical stance where you refer to what is good and also how things can be improved.

If the case study is to be followed by a presentation you should be given guidance on what you need to include.

Strategic analysis paper

When there is a need for candidates to demonstrate both strategic and creative thinking, a strategy paper might be provided along with a list of questions.

One particular example of this is called The Intrapreneurs. This comprises about one-and-a-half sides of detail on companies that have introduced this concept to develop ideas within their business, and instructions telling you what to do. This was used to recruit internal change agents. In this particular example the instructions were:

Candidate instructions

You have 1½ hours to complete the following tasks:

Read the case study – The Intrapreneurs.

Focusing on the Intrapreneurship programme, develop a mind map, fishbone diagram or similar to include both the stated and implied components of the programme. Consider what makes a good creative programme and conclude where intrapreneurship could be improved.

Develop a one-minute elevator speech to the marketing director of our company on your response to the questions 'Intrapreneurship – great idea, gets us away from all this boring process stuff. Turns all those drones into butterflies, why don't you start a programme?'

Given that you are forced to run such a programme, in overview what approach would you take?

Prepare for a 10-minute presentation. (Your notes will be returned to you a few minutes in advance of the presentation.)

Research analysis

Another written exercise could involve you being given two pieces of research, carried out by a management consultant. You would then need to prepare a written report, summarising what you see as the key points from the research and making a recommendation, for instance on where a new factory should be built. You need to go beyond being descriptive; you must analyse the data.

Client situation

A written case study will often be linked to a company's business, so if this is for a post in a law firm you might be given a real client problem and asked how you would advise the client.

 Often the company want to look beyond your professional knowledge to see if you also demonstrate commercial awareness. Reading the *Financial Times* or *The Economist* will be helpful.

Management situation exercise

This type of exercise presents you with a number of situations that you could face in a management role. You will be given a description of a particular situation and based on this information you have to say how you would handle it.

A typical situation is:

> You are involved in introducing a change to working practices, which will have a significant impact across the organisation. You also have a number of personal work projects which are all approaching a critical phase and you

are beginning to feel pushed to your limits, already working late each night. These past few weeks a number of senior managers have been in touch attempting to influence you on the changes you are trying to introduce. You don't have the time to deal effectively with their arguments. You have to make some decisions on how you will deal with these situations. What are you going to do?

With a limited amount of time, perhaps six situations to answer in 30 minutes, you will need to be brief and concentrate on the key issues as you only have five minutes to answer this.

TASK

Why not have a go now and see how much you can write, especially when this includes thinking time?

These exercises are often followed by a discussion to help understand the approach you took and the reasoning behind the actions you recommended. So for each situation you are likely to be asked:

- What was the key issue in each situation?

- What criteria did you use to make a recommendation?

- Why did you choose a particular recommendation over other possible options?

This could be followed by a general review:

- What approach did you take to this exercise?

- How effective was this approach?

- Would you do anything differently if you did this exercise again?

- Which was the most difficult situation and why?

Assessors will then review your answer to each situation. They will be checking that:

- You both identified and dealt with key issues
- Your actions were clear and you have made a recommendation
- Your actions will have improved the situation
- Your judgement was sound

Key tips

- When you answer the question do use short paragraphs and bullet points, it makes it easier for the assessors to read.
- There is unlikely to be a right answer, it is the reasoning that is of most importance.
- If you need to follow this with a presentation you could use your highlighter to mark the key points you want to make.

Chapter 11. In-tray exercises

In-tray exercises can provide excellent information for assessors to understand how you are likely to perform on the job. Whilst people can discuss at interview how they would handle a particular situation, as assessors we are never sure if this is how they would actually react if confronted with that scenario. Organisational skills and the ability to prioritise are important but so is being able to make a decision. The in-tray will show a candidate's ability to do both.

The in-tray also gives you, as the candidate, a taste of what to expect in the job. It's a work simulation covering the sorts of things you are likely to encounter if you are successful in the job, such as the different types of communication you will get and you deciding how to handle each one. This can include:

- **Requests** – how do you prioritise which gets done first?

- **Memos** – how will you deal with these?

- **Complaints or grievances** – how will you handle them?

Dependent on the job you are applying for, the focus will differ. For an administrative position the emphasis will be more on prioritisation. For a customer service job, how the person deals with conflict and manages people's expectations is key. For managers how you take action is vital; and for professionals the focus will be on your professional skills.

In-tray exercises are most commonly presented in e-tray format – you don't get a physical pile of papers but instead read documents on the screen, just like we do in our daily lives. Some companies may still be using a 'paper and pencil' version so I'll cover both.

In-tray exercises combine a number of documents for you to deal with – either on your desk or on the screen via your inbox. You also get supporting information in a folder of documents on your desk or online, sometimes both. This would include an outline of your role, time frame, an organisational chart and details of ongoing projects. Do refer to this so you know to whom you can delegate.

The majority of in-tray exercises follow the same scenario. You have a set amount of time to read through the items and you then need to make judgements. You are either new in your job or have just got back from holiday and your boss is away, so you need to make decisions without consulting others.

Watch out for conflicts, e.g. you need to be in two places at once, or there are pressing reasons why two people need the same week off but you can only give this to one person. How will you decide?

Paper and pencil in-tray exercises

On your desk you will find an in-tray and various items of stationery – headed paper, memo paper, forms to write down what you would have said on the phone if you had a phone available, etc.

They are specially designed so that some items are urgent and need immediate attention, others can only be dealt with when you get further information, and some items can go straight in the bin.

You will be given instructions including how much time you have and what you need to do – with each document you either deal with it, delegate it or leave it till later. If you delegate it you need to provide details on how you want the person to handle the item.

You are given a background document, for example:

> Today is Tuesday 4th January and it is 8.45am. Your name is Chris Watson and you are the manager of the

Birmingham office which employs 36 people as shown on the attached organisational chart.

You have been away from the office since Christmas Eve, spending time with family overseas and you kept your promise to your partner that you would not access work emails whilst away – you even left your work Blackberry at home. You left your assistant manager, Nicky Tallents, in charge during your absence. The Christmas period is normally quiet and Nicky is a very capable person.

You have arrived back to the in-tray that's in front of you. Every 30 minutes a messenger will call and collect outgoing messages and make deliveries of post and messages.

Generally the first thing you need to do is to go through each document and make a note of importance and urgency. There is never time to do everything and assessors want to see how you will manage your time.

You then need to make a decision on what to do with each document. You don't need to deal with everything yourself; you can forward some on for somebody else to deal with. Pay attention to what is most important and urgent and deal with these documents first of all.

Sometimes there is a link between documents, so look at all of them before replying. You can often get credit for a personal approach to each document, so mention the person by name and add your thanks. In addition, look for themes that run through the items, rather than treating each item individually.

E-tray exercises

The difference with an electronic e-tray exercise is that the different items will appear in your electronic intray. It's more like real life but as you can't print them out you may find it helpful to keep the documents open on the screen and saved but not sent as some subsequent emails may have an impact on earlier ones.

The technology is quite simple but you will be given a tutorial in advance to ensure you know what to do. Be clear about what is required – read the instructions and if you aren't sure ask. There is usually a practice exercise to help you. Instructions are available for you to review; if it's paper-based you can use your highlighter to indicate what is most important. The exercise gives you a scenario, so make sure you are clear on your roles and responsibilities for this exercise.

The in-tray is not always a standalone exercise; it is usually a prequel to a written exercise, often based on one or more of the items. For example, you may need to provide an in-depth response to one of the documents.

You will be told how long you have, and the time is likely to make the exercise quite demanding for you, so stay focused. Some exercises manage the time for you, such as 15 minutes reading, 40 minutes on the in-tray and 25 minutes for the written exercise. For others you need to manage your own time. They usually suggest how to split your time. It's useful to follow these guidelines because you need to make sure you do all of the tasks, and you won't do well with a brilliant e-tray but a written exercise that you've barely started.

You can take notes as you go through the exercise, both on paper and possibly on the computer as well (for the e-tray). It's unlikely that you will be able to cut and paste between documents.

There will be a set number of emails, often 20-30, but these won't all be in your inbox as you start the exercise. Just like in real life as you answer an email you will get a reply. So you can't wait and send off all your replies at the end. The emails you haven't read yet will show up in bold. There will also be additional documents which will be in a document folder on the screen, and provide useful supporting information. **You must refer to this as you answer each email and see how you can use this information in your reply.** When you click send, be confident in your answer as you won't be able to go back and change it once it has been sent.

 Some of the emails will have attachments, so look out for these. They are often included to check your attention to detail.

As you look at each email, you need to make a decision on how to answer it. Read through all the information carefully to make sure you fully understand the situation. Thinking of the possible implications of each response might help you decide what to do. Take account of the information in the attachment and information folder to help you make a decision.

Throughout keep track of the time and check how many emails you have answered and are left to answer. There is often a timer built into e-tray exercises, but just in case have your watch handy and note the start time. Also, some of the earlier emails may be more straightforward than later ones, which will take up more of your time.

Key points

- Read everything before acting as there is often something in one of the later items that will affect decisions on earlier ones.

- Look for patterns. There are often a number of items that are quite insignificant on their own but once brought together could indicate a more serious problem.

- Carefully review organisational charts, calendars, etc as these can be important.

- Be personable in the way you communicate, e.g. refer to people by name.

Chapter 12. Presentations

The presentation exercise can take many different forms. Some presentations are very short and given in front of other candidates, with minimal preparation time provided. Others can be made to one assessor, or possibly more, and if you are given the topic in advance you can spend as much time as you want on preparation. There are also other forms of presentations anywhere in between.

I want you to feel more confident with presentations, so let's share some examples from a range that I've either assessed or helped clients prepare for.

I'm dividing this chapter into three sections:

- five minute presentations to other candidates

- 10-20 minute presentation when you have limited preparation time

- 15-20 minute presentation when you have been able to prepare in advance

Five-minute presentations to other candidates

This sort of presentation can appear very scary – having to speak for three to five minutes in front of people you don't know. Companies use this type of exercise to get a feel for your personality (are you outgoing?) and also to see how you deal with a stressful situation.

The presentation can often be part of a group interview. For companies that get a lot of applicants this can be a cost-effective method of deciding who to take forward to a personal interview.

> The secret to being successful is having one or two prepared topics that you would be ready to talk about in any situation.

You usually get about five minutes to prepare and then need to be able to talk 'off the cuff' about a particular subject. So it helps if you have some things that you would be happy to talk about in any situation. You might have a love of fishing, or a passion for a historical figure. Perhaps you would be happy to discuss part of your gap year, or a difficult situation you overcame. You might also like to choose an example that relates to the key characteristics required in the job. Having one or two topics that you can talk about where you know you won't get flustered through not knowng what to say, can really help your confidence. What you must do, though, is **keep this preparation secret**; so don't make it sound too rehearsed, and actively use the thinking time to do just that and make some thoughtful notes.

Management trainee in a supermarket

Rob applied for a job in a large supermarket chain as a trainee manager. The first stage of the selection was a group interview. The second part was the individual presentations. Everyone was asked to talk for three minutes on a subject of their choice and had just five minutes to prepare.

Rob had discussed techniques with me and did exactly as outlined above. He had an example which demonstrated both his organisational skills and of him using his initiative, both of which were likely to be important for supermarket managers. His presentation was about an overseas trip he organised aged 18, for seven friends, and how he dealt with the situation when they arrived in a French town, their hotel rooms had been let go and it was 11pm at night.

10-20 minute presentation when you have limited preparation time

Many companies will ask you to prepare on the day, and all candidates will have the same amount of time to do so. The topic will probably be something you should have a view about as it is related to the job. Typical subjects include, 'how would you empower your team to high performance?' and 'with a competitor entering the market and our company's market share dropping by 20% what suggestions do you have to combat this?' You may be given access to the internet to help with your research.

A very common alternative approach is to be asked to present your results following an analysis of a case study.

Typically you would get between 30 minutes and an hour to prepare. Sometimes you will just need to have notes and not be expected to make a formal standing presentation, but in most circumstances you will have access to PowerPoint or a flip chart so you can prepare presentational aids.

What can help you get the best from this sort of situation is to practise giving a presentation with limited preparation time. Make sure you follow a typical structure such as:

- What the problem is

- Options available

- What you will do and why

- Conclusion

As part of your preparation you could think of a topic and prepare it under timed conditions. It doesn't matter if the topic comes up; just going through a timed exercise will be good preparation for you.

The most common presentation lasts 20 minutes so it can help to work out roughly how you will allocate your time. You might choose to have four slides and spend five minutes on each one. Or if you know you need less time for the conclusion you could put an extra 30 seconds into the other slides.

> You must keep track of time. When I have a candidate who has been given x minutes to present I expect them to use most of the time allowed. It's okay to be 10% under but if you use significantly less time you have missed out on a chance to impress the assessor. There should be a clock in the room, but don't rely on this and do take a watch so you can place it on the table in front of you to keep track of the time.

When you present ensure you make regular eye contact with the assessor and also have confidence in the way you present. You need to have a reasonable level of assertiveness and self-confidence, and try to project to the room.

If you do make use of PowerPoint, as in any other circumstances use the slides to make a point and to emphasise what you are saying, not to be a crib that you can read from.

Example candidate instructions

You are given 30 minutes to prepare a 10-minute presentation, and that includes producing any visual aids you require.

Imagine that you are a business consultant or advisor. One of your colleagues has been taken ill and you have to stand in for them and make a presentation to a group of local businesses who are interested in learning more about marketing for small businesses. Your talk is the main focus for their monthly meeting.

MS PowerPoint, flip charts and an OHP are likely to be available.

Tips

- Time is short and you might not get a chance to rewrite your copy so look for a way to make notes so you can easily add to your slides etc, if needs be.

- The tendency is for candidates to put all their notes on PowerPoint and then read them out loud, but this is a very boring presentational style and doesn't make a good impression on the assessor.

- A very sophisticated candidate would include items in the presentation that encouraged questions, and be ready with their replies. However, this can be hard to do under time constraints so be ready to think on your feet.

Some people love giving presentations but others are much more nervous, and these are often the more introverted candidates. Don't feel you have to be somebody you aren't, but just be a really good version of you. There's a TV advert for vitamins which says it makes you feel like you, but on a really good day! That's how you want to come across.

The follow on questions

Following your presentation you will be asked a number of questions. These will often include challenging you on the content, and you'll then be asked specific questions related to the approach you are recommending. Listen carefully to the question and be sure to answer it accurately. If you don't know the answer to a question it is better to say that rather than to guess.

You may also be asked how you approached the task and how you decided what the key message should be.

15-20 minute presentation when you have been able to prepare in advance

It sounds great. You have got the subject in advance so you can put in as much time as you like on your presentation. However, having been allowed more time the assessors will expect much more from you. You also have to think about how much time is sufficient. Preparing your presentation is just one part of your preparation to get the job, and you don't want to spend so much time on this that you forget to think abut how to answer interview questions or to have questions ready that you can ask.

Follow the advice in the section above but as you have plenty of time to prepare you will want to practise so you make full use of the time. Any slides you create will also need to look slick, with a careful choice of words.

> Think about the actual slides that you use and look to brand these as close as you can to the company you are applying to. For example, you could use the same colour scheme and include the company logo.

Think also about whether you will provide handouts to the assessor(s). This could be a set of PowerPoint handouts – three or six to a sheet – but you could also make yours stand out by creating a small A5 booklet, or by putting the key points on a double-sided sheet of high-quality paper, again branded like the slides.

A fairly common presentation is based around you having been successful in your application and for you to focus on what you plan to do in the job. For example, if you are applying for a job as a marketing manager at a university you could be asked to present on:

- The short, medium and long-term issues facing the university

- The implications of these issues for marketing within the faculties

- How you would develop and implement a faculty marketing strategy to support the university mission

You will be able to review information available on the company website and the company may also send you relevant details, in this case a copy of the company mission and values statement and the current marketing strategy and plan.

If you have been given 20 minutes then make sure you use the majority of the time allowed and don't overrun.

You can practise by reading silently to yourself, but it is much better to run through it like you will at the assessment centre. So stand up and speak with as little reference to your notes as possible. As your confidence increases get an audience, maybe your partner or friends, who will pick up on any ways that you can improve as well as telling you about your good points. Do tell your 'audience' that you seek feedback and that you want to hear about what went well, as well as ways you can improve.

How to structure a presentation

Introduction

- Introduce yourself and, if appropriate, your organisation, real or imaginary (you may be playing a sales manager for Company XYZ)

- Tell your audience what you are going to talk about, why they should listen to you, and how long you will talk for. Say that they are welcome to ask questions at the end (this enables the presentation to flow and the assessors can track your time better). You could say that you would be happy for questions during the presentation if they are of a technical nature and they don't understand something.

- Never apologise for your limited experience in making presentations

Delivery

- Use marker phrases such as 'the first point I would like to make', 'and finally' to reinforce the structure of your presentation

- Use simple words and avoid jargon

- Don't get bogged down in too much detail

- Summarise at the end of each section (if appropriate)

- Maintain eye contact with your audience and monitor their reaction. Is there a need for you to slow down, or become more formal in style?

- Appear confident, and this will give confidence to your audience

- Vary your voice tone and volume so you don't appear boring

Conclusion

- Flag up that you are coming to the end with a phrase such as 'to summarise' or 'in conclusion'

- Thank the audience for their attention

- Invite questions

Dealing with questions

- If you know the answer then reply clearly and succinctly

- If you don't know the answer, you could refer to your written material or put the question to the audience

- Some candidates turn the question back to the questioner, e.g. 'so what do you think the answer should be?', but an experienced assessor will put the question back to you and insist you answer

Review after a presentation

Some companies will ask you to review your performance either by completing a questionnaire or via an interview. Following a presentation you could be asked questions such as:

- How did you think it went?

- If you were going to do it again, would you do anything differently?

So be ready to comment. Don't think you need to put a positive spin on it; assessors are usually looking to make sure that your self-assessment is accurate and matches with that of the assessor.

Chapter 13. Role-plays

Role-plays are used by companies to see how well you are likely to perform in a particular situation that is relevant to the job. An experienced interviewee will say all the right things, but can they actually do what they say they can? That's why you may face a practical activity where you have to demonstrate your skills and abilities to respond to a particular situation.

In this chapter I'm going to talk you through six specific scenarios for different sorts of jobs, including customer service and professional and senior management positions. The advice I give is relevant to almost any role-play situation you may find yourself in.

As an assessor, many times I have had to take on the role of angry customer, recalcitrant employee, potential client and even a member of the media. Some assessors can be very good at this sort of task, and I think I may have missed my vocation as an actor, but others don't find it easy and it can also be difficult to both play a role and be the assessor, so professional actors are often used who have a script and can easily get into role.

> In a role-play exercise, it's not you that is playing a role but the assessor! You are being yourself in a situation which is likely to be relevant to the job, so treat the exercise as real, and show how well you can handle it.

1. Telephone customer service assistant

I worked as a consultant with one of the major mobile phone companies, helping them recruit call centre staff. In these jobs excellent customer relationship skills are essential – it's not enough for people to say that they are good with customers; we want examples of how they are likely to relate to them.

In this assessment centre, the role-play involved one candidate and two assessors. One assessor played the customer and the other assessor did the observation. We had the candidate and one assessor sitting back-to-back and they had to carry out a conversation 'as if' they were on the phone. The candidate was given some information to read in advance, just one sheet of paper, covering basic information for answering customer calls. They didn't need to memorise everything as they could take the sheet of paper into the room with them, but they needed to be able to access it quickly. This is one reason why I always recommend that you take your own highlighter pen with you, just in case one isn't provided.

The assessor was also given a script and told how to behave (we had been briefed on this as part of the training we undertook in advance of the assessment centre). When playing a 'difficult customer' it is important not to be too difficult and to be consistent between sessions so that some candidates don't have an easier task than others.

What we noticed was that some candidates couldn't adapt to the task, and this is an important part of doing well – you have to think of yourself as, in this example, a call centre advisor. It's useful to do this anyway as part of your preparation for an interview or assessment centre as it helps you to prepare for possible questions.

The assessor would start with 'ring, ring' and the candidate was told to answer the phone in the standard way for the company. This is easy – you are just saying what is written down – but there are still ways to do this well (and badly). Think about the tone of your voice, make yourself sound friendly and interested, this sets the tone for the discussion. This is an essential aspect of a customer service job and if you don't want to be warm and friendly with people why are you applying for the job?

The assessor (as customer) then relays their problem and wants to see how the candidate (as call centre advisor) responds. In such an exercise this isn't going to be overly complicated, you just need to be able to use some key information as you talk to the customer.

Overall, as assessors what we want is for you as the call centre advisor to:

- Leave the customer with a positive experience

- Be seen as somebody who listens to what is said (so summarising is helpful)

- Show some empathy and concern for the situation, but don't necessarily admit blame

- Reach a conclusion, even if it is that you need to find out more and get back to them. In which case confirm the customer's contact details

- Be mindful of the time. You will have been told how long you have for this exercise so stay within the time allowed, and remember these sorts of jobs rely on customers being dealt with promptly to meet the performance indicators for the task

Customer service assistant (CSA)

A similar type of role-play is used for a job as a customer service assistant, dealing with large crowds of people. In this particular situation empathy is important but there is also a need for assertiveness. Many people think of assertiveness as getting your own way, particularly at the expense of others, but that is being aggressive. Assertiveness is more about being clear on what you want and need to do, but also paying attention to other people's point of view.

The exercise we used on this occasion was for the candidate to play the role of a CSA who was working at a train station and had to hold people at a barrier for safety reasons. As an assessor I had to play a 'difficult customer' who was late for a meeting and didn't appreciate the reasons why the CSA reacted as they did.

The candidates brief said to focus on the instructions 'to hold people back for safety reasons' and if the customer showed anger or frustration then to be unhelpful. However, if they calmed down you could then show some empathy and understanding and reassure them that the situation would be resolved in the next 10 minutes.

2. Consultancy/client relationship jobs

These types of jobs are usually at a higher level and involve building more long-term relationships. They could involve roles where you will be a consultant or an advisor to companies, which is partly about building relationships but also winning the business.

Let's look at one particular example, that of a candidate applying for a job as a marketing manager. The candidate brief would give you a scenario, rather than provide an actual brief. It would tell you your role, that you have a meeting and what the meeting should achieve.

Candidate brief

You are the marketing manager at the University of XYZ. You have to plan for a meeting with the Head of School and form a relationship with them in order to convey the need for marketing.

You would get a brief containing background information and timings, for example 20 minutes to prepare and 30 minutes for the meeting. This could be actual company material.

The brief will tell you the purpose of the meeting, which is to:

- Build a positive working relationship

- Assess their current marketing needs

- Explain why there is a need for marketing

- Present your marketing ideas (based on the information in the brief)

- Agree the next steps

After your preparation you will go into the meeting, which will probably last for 20-30 minutes.

Role-player/assessor brief

The role-player gets a detailed brief to help them 'get into role'. Naturally their brief will be at odds with the information given to you as a candidate. He/she is likely to be preoccupied with other thoughts and meeting the marketing manager is not top of his/her priorities.

Often a role-player is told to be difficult but not too difficult, and they can be persuaded as long as you in your role as marketing manager put some effort into this. In this sort of scenario the person usually doesn't see the need for marketing and will be focused (in the above example) on the more academic aspects of their work. If you are sufficiently convincing then you are likely to win the role-player around, or at least get them thinking about what you suggest.

You will of course have a plan, but it is also important to listen to what the role-player has to say and to make sure that you hear and respond to their concerns, just don't forget your own objectives.

The role-player is sometimes focused on something that is irrelevant to your objective, in this case perhaps a paper they are to present at an important overseas conference, so recognising how important this is to them, and spending some time listening to them, will then allow you to focus on your objective for the meeting.

Ask probing questions that start with how, why, when, where and what, which will get the role-player talking so you then know how best to respond. Do use active listening skills so you hear what the person has to say and can respond accordingly.

3. People management jobs

Most management jobs involve you having to manage staff and this can be quite difficult for some, particularly when moving from a technical to team-leader role. So if you are, for example, an experienced IT professional how easy will it be for you to make the transition to team leader?

When assessing for people management roles we are not always expecting perfection, but we do want to see the underlying natural ability of a candidate to work with people and to what extent they can bring out the best in others through coaching and motivational skills.

Frequently the role-play will be structured around a situation where you are the manager and you have a 'problem' member of staff. Often they are not performing well on the job, perhaps some negative feedback has been received by the company or co-workers have complained.

If you are applying for a people management job you should feel comfortable managing people and should have already given some thought to how you would manage others. Useful preparation is to think through possible scenarios and I have included some in this section.

You are likely to be given e.g. 15 minutes to read through any information and to prepare. The assessors will enter the room and sit quietly; do ignore them! There will then be a knock on the door and the role-player will walk in. The meeting will then start and you must make sure you finish within the allocated time (generally 25-30 minutes).

A typical scenario is to give you a brief outlining a situation. It will revolve around a named member of staff who will often be played by a professional actor. 'Chris' is the name often used as it's unisex. They will also have been given a script to follow. A benefit of using a professional actor is that they can quickly get into character and can maintain a similar position across perhaps four or even six role-play sessions. The scenarios could include:

- Chris has been working for you for a couple of years and he has been getting poor internal feedback on the work he has been doing for customers.

- Chris is in a sales role and has yet to hit her sales targets despite being in the role for three months.

- Chris has been a great worker but of late his work has deteriorated. He also appears scruffy and people have commented on his personal hygiene. It has been suggested that he might have an alcohol-related problem.

- Chris is unmanageable. She just doesn't listen to the things you have asked her to do and is facing disciplinary proceedings. This will be the last meeting before you go down the disciplinary path.

In all of these situations you want to ask an open question at the beginning to get the person talking and also demonstrate that you are listening to what they have to say. There is often an underlying personal problem that is affecting their work, and they may not share this information with you immediately. The role-player brief will tell them not to volunteer information unless you have developed a reasonable working relationship with them.

It can certainly be helpful for you to summarise what has been said and to have clear actions for you and them to take. You also want to make sure that the person you manage has shown commitment to the action.

After the role-play you will often be asked to make a note on how you found the exercise, and to what extent you thought you did well, or not. Don't feel you have to be overly positive, but do aim to be accurate. If you know you did well, say so, but if you can think of what you could have done better it is worth making a note of it. It's often once something is over that we realise a different approach would have been more effective. As an assessor I will be seeing to what extent the candidate's self-assessment matches with what I've observed, and if a candidate is accurate, even if they recognise they have done poorly, they will score better (on a competence of learning and improving) than an overly harsh or positive assessment.

How best to prepare

- Think about different possible work situations, such as those above, and think through how you would deal with them.

- Talk to other people and ask for their opinions.

- Look for opportunities to develop some actual experience; you could do this working with a voluntary organisation.

4. Coach/counsellor/interviewer/training jobs

When recruiting people for a job as a coach, counsellor, interviewer or trainer, assessors are unlikely to make a decision just because somebody says that they are good at it. We also want to get some evidence of how they will actually coach someone, run a training session, etc.

Role-players will be used, and again there will be more than one person in the room with you. One of them will be the client, or the 'group' you are training.

When faced with this situation, try to forget that this is an assessed interview and focus on the client, doing exactly what you would normally do in a client situation. Candidates that do poorly will often blame the exercise, they say that it wasn't 'real', but, particularly when role-players are used, this situation is very close to a real life situation. However, I do recognise that there are some differences:

- **Duration:** Instead of a typical 50-60 minute session you only have 20-30 minutes.

- **Limited introduction:** You can't go into a long introduction so you have to cover this much more quickly.

To do well make sure that you cover the basics – tell the 'client' about time availability, confidentiality, note taking, offer a glass of water, etc. Do take some notes as you talk as you may need to write a summary at the end and these should help. Sometimes you may not know how to summarise, or feel a bit confused and one way of dealing with this is to ask the client to sum up the discussion.

If you have to run a training session it might seem a little odd to be training just one person. One approach is to pretend that there are lots of people in the room and to address questions to a wider audience. The assessor(s) is looking to see if you can present well, but as many training sessions involve facilitation you can also involve the audience by asking questions and encouraging some group working.

5. Peer role-play

The role-play may focus on how you work with other people at the same level as you in an organisation. This could be assessed in a group exercise, with four or six people addressing a topic, but it could also be done on a one-to-one basis with an assessor or role-player taking on the role of a peer.

You will have time to prepare and be given relevant information to read. This is often related to previous exercises and builds on, for example, the in-tray exercise.

The brief will have told you the purpose of the meeting – to share information and reach a decision. So be clear on what is important, what you want to achieve, what the most important parts of the argument are and also where you can be flexible. However, new information may come from the role-player so you must be flexible enough to adapt.

Again an assessor, as observer, may be in the room with you. If so, ignore them and give all your attention to your peer. At the end of the meeting you will probably need to draft a memo to your manager summarising the situation.

6. Dealing with the press

If you are being assessed for a director's job, particularly in a large company, you may face a role-play exercise where you are being interviewed by a TV or radio interviewer. When I worked for the Post Office we used a highly experienced press officer to conduct an interview with people applying for top jobs as we wanted to assess how well they would present themselves should they have to face this situation. This would usually occur because there has been a major incident, e.g. an accident or a strike, and we wanted to see how well the candidate could stand up against quite pressurised interviewing. I've also done similar exercises with a large transport organisation, where the aspiring director had to respond to questioning following a serious accident.

All the examples I've discussed have been role-plays involving the candidate and one other person. Very occasionally role-plays may involve two other people; this is usually to see how you are likely to react when there is conflict between two people, or when you have to quickly assess which is the most important task to deal with, such as if you work with the emergency services. This can be quite stressful so stay calm and make sure that you are clear on what you need to do.

Before the assessment centre

Think about the job you are applying for and the sort of one-to-one situation you might find yourself in. Then you could practise a role-play with a friend. For example, if you are applying for a job which involves customer service skills, ask your friend to play a difficult customer and see how you are able to deal with the particular situation. You can then both debrief afterwards.

Key tips

- Be clear on your role in the scenario
- Carefully read all the information provided
- Have some clear objectives and outcomes for the meeting and keep track of how you are doing
- Think about what is likely to be most important and make sure that this is discussed
- Plan, but don't be too focused on your plan, you may need to adapt to the unexpected
- Be willing to speak up and don't give up at the first sign of pressure
- Be ready for objections and think of how you can best address them – you can always say 'can we park this?' and move on
- How can you best work with the role-player? Make sure you can adapt to suit different people's personalities and working styles
- Ask open questions to get the other person talking using what, when, why, who, where and how, and then listen to what they say
- Don't forget to keep track of time
- Most role-plays will benefit from you summarising what was discussed and agreeing next steps, including the date of a next meeting

Chapter 14. Other exercises

The previous chapters have covered the most common activities included in an assessment centre, but there is always a chance of some others. Please don't be fazed, remember the activities are chosen to relate to the job you are applying for, and if you don't enjoy the task you probably won't enjoy the job.

Research challenge

If the job you are applying for involves research you may be given a task that demonstrates how well you can find out information, again under tight time constraints.

In this type of interview you will be asked to go and find something out. For example, if you are applying for a junior researcher role you may be given access to a phone and a computer and asked to find a particular expert.

If you are faced with a research task, make sure you understand what is required of you. The question may be purposely confusing to assess whether you fully understand the task.

Fact-finding interviews

If the job you are applying for requires you to find out information – e.g. working as a police officer, loss adjustor or tax inspector – then a fact-finding exercise could be included in the assessment centre. You would be given a brief description of a scenario and you would then have perhaps just five minutes to identify pertinent questions.

It's hard to think of questions under time pressure so remember to use the '5 Ws and an H' – what, where, who, why, when and how. Write your questions down, and leave space for the answers.

You will then have around 20 minutes to conduct the interview. Don't forget about developing rapport and also listen carefully! Their answers will be prompts for more questions. Make a note of the answers; you won't be able to hold all the information in your head.

You will then need to review the answers and make a decision. It's not as simple as counting up the evidence for and against, because you must also weight the evidence; some items will be more important than others. You then present your results to an assessor. In this meeting you might be given more information and may be asked if you want to change your decision.

Before the assessment centre

You need to make sure you can ask open questions, to get the other person talking. So pay attention to the questions you ask others. You don't want to ask closed questions which require a yes or no answer, 'Did you see him enter the building?', nor do you want to ask multiple questions, 'How many people would you say were in the room, and what time of day was it?' as you are likely to just get one of the questions answered. Don't ask leading questions either.

You can prepare by reading through the first paragraph of a news story and giving yourself five minutes to make a note of as many questions as you can. Then read the rest of the article and see how many of your questions were answered.

You could also conduct a meeting with someone who is knowledgeable about a subject that you know little about – bee-keeping, historical re-enactment, off-road driving, etc. Make a list of questions, then have a 15-minute meeting, and afterwards ask the person to tell you about any obvious questions you missed.

Planning and scheduling exercises

If you are applying for a job as a project or logistics manager you may need to complete a planning and scheduling exercise. This has a clear relevance to the job, and so this would allow you to demonstrate your strengths. You would be given details on the task and resources available (people, equipment, budget) to help you decide how to fulfil the task.

If you are applying for this sort of job you should be clear on the steps needed to complete a project:

- Define the objectives and deadline

- Identify all tasks to be completed and the required resources

- Order the tasks which needs to be done first

- Estimate how long each task will take, including start and finish dates

- Complete the tasks according to the plan

- Review progress and amend as necessary

It is imperative that you read the instructions carefully, and it can be helpful to highlight key points. Make sure that you create a rough plan before you start and manage your time to make sure you can complete it.

Before the assessment centre

If you are rusty or less familiar with project management then read a simple project management book. Also go through the steps to plan a large family party or a house move as that will enable you to use the necessary technique in a more familiar area.

Manual tasks

For some specific jobs you may need to demonstrate your manual dexterity. Several years ago I worked on a large assessment process where employees were assessed for their suitability for retraining into alternative career paths. For one technical job this included using small and delicate equipment, and also seeing if someone was colour-blind by asking them to choose the right coloured cables from a large bundle.

If the job you are applying for does not need manual skills then these won't be assessed.

Keyboard skills test

If you are applying for a job that requires good keyboard skills you should expect to do a test that demonstrates your skills.

I haven't been an employee for over 12 years, and back then most secretaries were not very good at using the Microsoft Office package. I needed my PA to be able to produce presentational materials using PowerPoint and to use advanced features on Microsoft Word, so I constructed a task for people to produce some materials for me. Thus I could find out if they had the skills I needed. I can still see this sort of test being relevant even now.

Filing test

If you are applying for an administrative job where a high attention to detail is needed an exercise you might be asked to undertake is to do some filing. The assessors will be checking how much you do within the time, as well as levels of accuracy. I would certainly put more weight on being accurate. John had to do a test like this when he applied for a job with a health authority. The filing test involved putting files in alphabetical order and some files had first names first, rather than the surname and this could have tripped up some candidates.

Key tips

- Understand the requirements of the job as that helps you anticipate what you might be asked to do.

- Read the instructions carefully and make sure you understand what you need to do.

- If there is a need to be accurate, slow down to increase your chance of getting things correct.

- For any task involving people, listen carefully and ask open questions.

Interviews

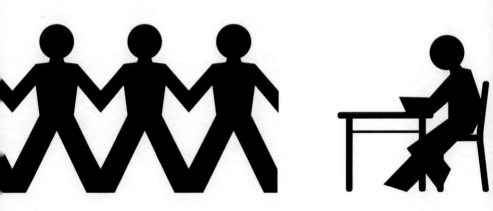

Chapter 15. The interview – preparation

Whether you have been shortlisted for 'just' an interview or a full assessment centre, the information in this chapter will be useful. Don't forget the company already think you can do the job, otherwise you wouldn't have been shortlisted. You will also have submitted a great application form, which is likely to have included some specific research on the job, company and industry.

Now's a good time to review your application and make sure that you feel confident to answer the various questions you might be asked. But before we move onto this, let's take a step back and make sure you are clear on what sort of interview you are facing.

An interview is the most familiar method of selecting people for a job but too often people don't do themselves justice. They haven't done the research and they don't know how to present themselves well.

I've interviewed literally thousands of people for a range of jobs and companies. Some people are modest, others nervous and then there are those who are too direct and are 'too much talk and too little substance'.

The interviewers vary too, from the highly professional to those with limited training who will make up their mind about you before you answer specific questions. This chapter will include suggestions on what to say when faced with an inexperienced interviewer.

The letter inviting you for interview should explain the type of interview you will face. There are many different sorts, from a short screening to a comprehensive one-hour competency-based interview and this could be one-to-one or with a panel of up to a dozen people.

Types of interview

Screening

This is usually with a recruitment consultant and is often quite short. They want to check you match with the information you have put on your application form. At this sort of interview provide clear and factual answers.

Panel

This could be with two or three people to eight or more. This type of interview is often used when a decision is taken by a large number of people who all want to see you, but they won't all be skilled interviewers. It reduces the risk of bias and allows more people to observe the applicant; however it can be quite stressful and harder for a candidate to develop rapport. In this situation you need to identify who holds the power (they often sit in the middle) and provide good eye contact with them. As you answer focus most on the person who asked the question but also be sure to make eye contact with the whole panel.

Formal one-to-one or two-to-one

This usually has you sat across a desk and is conducted in a very business-like manner with little encouragement provided. You need to be quite formal in your replies and to think around the question they ask you as they are unlikely to help you out if you don't give sufficient detail.

Informal

This is usually undertaken sat on comfy chairs with a coffee table between you, or sat at a desk but at right angles. The aim is to relax you, as when candidates are more relaxed they are more likely to be open. Beware, though, the interviewer who has you so relaxed that you become a bit too open! Remember that however informal the setting, you're still being interviewed.

Biographical

This takes a semi-structured approach through your life, based on the premise that past behaviour predicts future behaviour. The style is what candidates expect – being asked questions about their work, education and personal life – but it's used less now, with the competency-based interview being more popular.

Competency-based

This is a structured interview where questions are asked based on job-related competences, hence this style of questioning is well suited to an assessment centre. Candidates can use examples from different aspects of their life, not just work-related ones. It does give an advantage to articulate candidates, particularly those who have been coached in how to answer these questions.

Situational

This is a series of job-related questions where your responses are compared to those considered to be experts in the job. It is often used for phone interviewing as a means of shortlisting. Candidates tend to like these questions as they appear highly relevant to the job.

Group

This is a cross between an interview and a group exercise, but it's closer to an interview. It is often used by a company who has a lot of applicants, as a means of getting an initial opinion of who they want to see for a more detailed interview.

Richard told me about the way that he was recruited for one of the chains of motorway service stations. Anyone who applied could get a group interview and these were held on a weekly basis. The head of HR would give a short talk and the candidates were then split into smaller groups where, for about 30 minutes, they were asked work-related questions. These were not targeted at individuals but asked to the group. If you had the confidence to speak up you were more likely to be shortlisted than if you were shy and a bit hesitant.

Second

At a second interview, whilst the company will be interested in what you have done there will be much more focus on what you can offer the company. You must show warmth, energy, commitment and competence. You will be expected to have a quick grasp of the issues and to speak with confidence. Don't forget to review your notes from the first interview beforehand.

Problem solving

Years ago, when I worked for the Post Office, the assessment centres included a problem-solving interview which covered three topics: one with a connection to an applicant's work or background, one neutral and one stretching. These types of questions are still used by other companies, often as a second interview alongside a competency one. These topics would be on subjects such as:

- Imagine you have been tasked with project-managing the transfer of a large distribution centre from Glasgow to Inverness; talk me through how you would do this.

- The government have decided that to bring us in line with Europe as a country we should move to driving on the right-hand side of the road. If you were in charge tell me how you would do this.

If you face this type of interview treat it like a project. Before you get into the detail of implementation first consider options by coming up with ideas. Through questioning you will be taken into more detail.

Case

The case interview is similar to a case study but instead of writing things down you debate the topic with an assessor, hence it shares some similarities to the problem-solving interview above. The assessor wants to see how well you can present your case. If you don't like this type of interview you are unlikely to be well-suited to the job it is testing you for.

As a consultant you need to listen carefully to a client, and ask questions to help you work out how best to help them. There is not necessarily a right or wrong answer, but you need to ask questions, analyse the answers and decide how best to reply. Problems could include how to get a new product to market, what to do about falling profits, etc.

The information to analyse could include numerical data, so you must be able to calculate averages and percentages without a calculator. Whilst this is an interview, you could still take some notes, so it is useful to have your own pen and paper just in case none is available. As you ask questions you could note down key points, but don't write more than is necessary.

Puzzle

These types of interviews are similar to the sort of problems you may discuss in the pub with your geeky friends!

- How would you weigh a jet without using scales?

- Why are manhole covers round instead of square?

- You have a three-pint bucket, a five-pint bucket, and an infinite supply of water. How can you measure out exactly four quarts?

- Suppose you go home, enter your house, go to switch the lights on and nothing happens – no light floods the room. What are the steps you would take in determining what the problem was?

Companies use these sorts of questions to see how creative an applicant is and how well they can think creatively when under stress. Microsoft is known for using this approach and apparently other companies will also use this technique because Microsoft does!

This is certainly a good way of finding out how creative someone is, which may be an essential element of a job. This type of questioning is unlikely to be used in roles that do not require creative thinking. The answers to many puzzle questions are available on the internet and some candidates may do better than they otherwise would have simply because they have researched the answers. However, this does demonstrate research skills and preparation!

In many cases getting the right answer is less important than demonstrating your approach and how you analyse a problem, so if you get these questions, stay calm and think clearly and creatively.

Expectations

Interviews are not always what you expect. That's why you need to understand the different types so you are ready should you find yourself in a different situation than you were anticipating.

Simon had been invited to a competency-based panel interview – that was what was on his letter of invite and what we had prepared for. That's not what he got! Later he described a very general interview. The first question was, 'explain the gaps in your application form when you say that you were not working or studying?' and the next, 'if you are stuck in a lift for 5 minutes with a member of parliament, what one aspect of British foreign policy would you suggest they change?' Alongside the more typical 'why do you want the job' questions. Luckily he was able to adapt to the questions asked, but for someone else it might have been a bit disconcerting.

Key preparation

There are certain areas that you should always prepare:

1. How to answer the question 'tell me a bit about yourself'

2. Be clear on your strengths and weaknesses

3. Research the job, the company and industry

4. Answers to typical questions

1. How to answer to the question 'tell me a bit about yourself'

This is one of the most common questions you can be asked and one where so many candidates let themselves down. The really great thing about this question is that you can prepare in advance and it gets the interview off to a great start.

It's not unknown for interviewers to have to see 10 people in a day so they may not have properly read your paperwork. Asking this question helps the interviewer be clear on who they have in front of them. As interviewers we also ask this as we want to hear what you think are the key pieces of information that you want to share.

You only need to talk for a couple of minutes but should cover four areas:

1. **An introductory sentence to get the interviewer used to your voice.** I'm not Welsh and interviewed someone with a strong Swansea accent recently; it certainly took time to tune in to her very fast mode of talking.

2. **A short summary of yourself and your achievements.** What are the highlights that you want to share? What makes you stand out? Why are you applying for this job?

3. **A brief history of your previous employment.** Concentrate on some key achievements and your most recent jobs.

4. **A concluding statement.** Make it clear you have finished, perhaps by asking, 'would you like me to tell you any more on anything I've said?'

2. Be clear on your strengths and weaknesses

The second most popular question is to ask you about your strengths and weaknesses. This normally comes towards the end of the interview. Interviewers want to know which are your strengths and why, so think about these in advance, and give an example to demonstrate them. Instead of saying, 'I'm good at organising' say something like, 'I'm known as someone who is highly organised. Recently I set up a party for 80 people dealing with everything from catering, entertainment and contingency planning.'

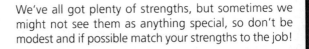

We've all got plenty of strengths, but sometimes we might not see them as anything special, so don't be modest and if possible match your strengths to the job!

You also must be able to refer to some weaknesses. Interviewers have heard the 'I don't suffer fools gladly' example far too many times, so think about something you have overcome, or an issue that is less relevant to the job. Also include how you conquered this weakness or how you manage it. For example, if you struggle to spot errors when proof-reading explain how you get someone else to check through important documents. This may well accompany strengths of being very creative or strategic.

3. Research the job, the company and industry

In Chapter 2 we discussed how to get as much detail as you can from the company, in addition to being clear about why you applied and why you are going to be perfect for the job. You then need to find out as much as you can about the company, and also research the industry. This means you can ask intelligent questions, plus it gives you a psychological advantage.

4. Answers to typical questions

Although there are some questions you are likely to get, which you'll find in the next chapter, you must also be aware that you could get some bizarre ones too (such as puzzle interviews see page 178). You may also be faced with someone who frankly should never be allowed to interview, as they certainly aren't trained.

You may discover that they don't have a plan and even are unsure of what to ask, so help them out by asking if, for example, they would like you to talk about your experience of project management.

Most interviewers will ask open questions and encourage you to answer the questions, but some interviewers are less easy to work with and you may face interviewers who ask closed questions, monopolise the interview or are inexperienced. Here are some ways to respond:

- **The interviewer asks only closed questions.** A closed question demands just a yes or no answer, such as 'Do you have any experience of winning business?', but you must treat it like an open question and say something like, 'Yes I have won business. To give you an example I presented to Company XYZ and this resulted in winning a contract to run six two-day training events over a three-month period, and I won this against strong competition'.

- **The interviewer monopolises the interview.** It's said that the more an interviewer talks, the more they like the candidate, but you want to be able to give them relevant examples for when they make their decision. To do so you need to be quite firm and speak once they pause for breath, saying something like, 'I can give you an example of how I have done that; at my previous company I...'

- **You are faced with a very inexperienced interviewer.** When I trained assessors they went through a five-day pass or fail course and had four assessed practice interviews. If they were not good enough they had to work with an experienced interviewer before they could go it alone. Most companies are not like this and some people are put to interviewing after just half a day's training. It's no wonder that some interviewers have done little preparation, run out of questions and don't know how to follow up. Accordingly, you need to look for ways to help them out. You can refer the interviewer to examples on your CV and also provide more details on what you have already discussed. For example, you could say, 'When talking about my experience at ... was it clear that...' or 'When I was describing what I did at ... I should have added...'

- **The interviewer asks multiple questions:** Some interviewers will ask two questions in one, e.g. 'Would you be interested in the training aspect of this work, and do you have any experience in writing course materials?' It's very easy to forget the other part of the question, so repeating it aloud as part of your reply should help.

We can now move onto preparing in more depth how to answer questions.

Chapter 16. Getting ready to answer questions

There are many questions you could be asked, and no one can know exactly what these will be, but thinking through answers to particular questions will help and you can often use this preparation to answer other questions.

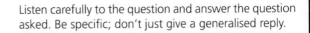

Listen carefully to the question and answer the question asked. Be specific; don't just give a generalised reply.

If you want this job – and, if not, why are you going for it, then you need to prepare. By understanding as much as you can about the requirements of the job, you can think of examples that are going to be relevant. And that way you aren't just going to have to hope that the interviewer can spot the connection – you have made it for them.

In this chapter we will firstly look at how to answer competency-based questions, which are the most popular sort used at assessment centres. You can also use this approach to answer more general questions covered in the second half of this chapter, and your interviewer will find a structured and focused response very helpful.

Competency-based interviews

Many interviewers follow a competency-based approach to interview questions. These are always used within assessment centres as they can match closely to the other exercises, which are always marked against competences. The types of questions you could get asked include:

- Can you recall a situation where you had to demonstrate your skills in problem solving? What was the problem and how did you tackle it?

- Can you give an example of when you have had to quickly build effective working relationships with someone?

The best way to prepare is to use the STAR approach for your examples. You need to describe the **Situation** you were in, the **Task** you were asked to accomplish, the **Action** you took and why, and the **Results** of your actions. This will help the interviewer follow your account and see your accomplishments.

STAR example

'Can you give me an example of when you have had to deal with a difficult interpersonal situation?'

Situation: When I started my last job I became Jim's manager; Jim had also applied for the job.

Task: I needed to quickly build a good working relationship and to recognise the sensitivity needed to work with someone who had been covering the job temporarily and was now feeling disengaged.

Action: To begin with I made sure that Jim knew I appreciated his knowledge and expertise and that as a new manager part of my role was to help develop him in his career.

Result: It certainly wasn't easy but through asking Jim about his career goals and recognising what he did well, I was able to identify ways that I could help him to be more effective in his weaker areas.

As an interviewer I would also ask follow-up questions to get more detail on a candidate's answer, but some interviewers have a set of questions and don't deviate from this list. I don't think this is good practice, but just in case, it's best to provide sufficient detail and if necessary to ask whether you can add some more to that question if they move you onto the next one when you can still think of more to say.

When a company develops a list of competences (their competency framework) these will include a key word or phrase such as 'tenacity' or 'planning and organising', and also a series of indicators which are used to create a list of questions. For example:

Analysis and use of evidence consists of:

- Gathering and managing information
- Innovating
- Generating and evaluating options
- Making well-judged decisions
- Linking work to its impact on society

If you get the detail against each competence you can use these indicators to develop possible questions – that's what the interviewer will be doing. If not you need to think about what sorts of questions you could be asked.

I'm going to include a number of examples in this section which you can then use to help you with further possible competences.

You will see in the competences below that they are sometimes grouped together, such as communicating and influencing. This is not always the case; sometimes they are treated individually and sometimes they are combined differently, such as influencing grouped with leading.

Competences

Against the following competences I want you to think of a specific answer that you would give to each question. The question may be asked quite directly, or it might be in a less direct way such as, 'At times we all find it difficult to work with some people; can you give me an example of when you have found it difficult to build an effective working relationship with someone?' The reason I phrase a question this way is to encourage a candidate to answer, as I'm suggesting that we all have problems at times.

Working with others

This is a very common competence so you need to be ready to answer questions in a number of areas. Questions could relate to the following areas, so think of examples you could use, and use STAR (see page 186) to structure your answer and make sure you cover everything. You probably would only be asked three or four questions, but we don't know which ones so more preparation will help.

- Tell me about a time when you have built effective working relationships with others.

- Tell me about a time when you have worked as part of a team to achieve an objective.

- Tell me about a time when you have worked with people very different to you.

- Give me an example of when you found it difficult to build effective working relationships with customers or colleagues.

- Tell me about a time when you have had to relate to more senior people in your organisation.

- How do you respond when there is conflict between team and personal goals?

Communicating and influencing

Competences can sometimes be combined, as in this example, but they could also be treated separately. Communication could also include questions related to both verbal and written skills.

- Tell me about a time when you have presented information clearly.

- Can you give me an example of communicating ideas across and beyond your organisation?

- Tell me about a time when you won someone over to your point of view.

- Give me an example of when you have had to appear credible in front of a group of people.

- Give me an example of when you have found it difficult to persuade someone to come round to your point of view.

- Tell me of a time when you have had to influence a key decision-maker.

Leading and managing

These two often go together, even though leadership and management are not the same; make sure you are clear on the difference and have examples of both. This could include work and non-work examples:

- Please give me an example of when you have had to delegate important work to others.

- Please give me an example of managing a group of people in order to achieve a particularly important outcome.

- Please give me an example of helping a person achieve business objectives.

- Tell me about a time when you have had to take responsibility for a group of people.

Analysing and problem-solving

Many jobs involve being able to analyse data and solve problems. At an assessment centre this will be assessed through the written exercise but may also be included in the interview, often to check on your ability to respond to quick questions.

- Please give me an example of when you have had to solve a challenging problem.

- Please give me an example of when you have had to make a decision based on objective analysis of data.

- Please give me an example of when you have asked probing questions to discover an underlying issue.

Planning and organising

If the job involves an element of planning and organising, then alongside a planning exercise you will also face questions about your experience.

- Please give me an example of when you have had to work to meet a deadline.

- Please give me an example of when you have had to organise time and resources to complete a project.

- How do you handle the routine elements of your work?

- Please give me an example of when you have missed a deadline.

- Please give me an example of when you have had to juggle a number of different activities at the same time.

Strategic thinking

As we apply for more senior roles, strategic thinking becomes more important, and this can be a difficult change for many; it takes a broader perspective and many struggle as they move from middle to senior management.

- Please give me an example of making sure you have the right information for making strategic decisions.

- Tell me how you make sure you keep up-to-date with organisational issues that could affect your decision-making.

- Explain how you have demonstrated a clear vision to achieve a business goal.

- Please give me an example of making suggestions to improve working practices.

- Can you talk me through how you solved a complex problem (this is asked to see if you answer from a strategic or operational level).

Coping with pressure and setbacks

Resilience is an important personal quality, and companies like to employ people who have it. So the questions provide information for them to judge how well you are likely to deal with challenging situations.

- Please give me an example of when you have worked under significant pressure.

- Please give me an example of when things have gone wrong and you have felt like giving up.

- Please give me an example of being given feedback you thought was unfair.

- Please give me an example of when you have had to cope with competing demands.

- Tell me how you recovered from a setback.

Using your initiative

Companies want employees who can use their initiative at all levels. Not waiting to be told what to do, but making suggestions and taking ownership.

- Please give me an example of when you took personal responsibility for a piece of work or project.

- Please tell me about the goals you have for your future.

- Please give me an example of when you have taken the initiative to change a process or procedure.

> The examples you give must be your own examples, not something you have copied from somebody else. If you don't have an example from work, look to your hobbies and outside interests, as they are still relevant.

Other interview questions

These are more general questions, but using the STAR approach will also be helpful to give your answer some structure.

Tell me about yourself?

We covered this in the previous chapter, so you should feel comfortable answering this one.

Why have you applied for this job?

Avoid the temptation to say what you will gain – a job, the training, or the perks! Instead, focus on what you have learnt about the company and how it is a great match for your skills, abilities and personal qualities. You can use the information you have found from your research, such as the company being a market leader, the way the company gets involved with local initiatives, etc.

What do you know about us?

In Chapter 2 we discussed the importance of research. You will use this knowledge to answer this particular question, thus making you stand out from the majority of candidates, who have failed to do so. Some interviewers may really pursue how much you have found out with questions such as:

- What does our organisation do?

- What do you think of our website?

- Who do you think are our major competitors?

- What or who do you think is the main threat to our business?

- What do you think of our product/service?

- What do you think are the main issues for our business over the next few years?

So make sure you can answer these questions.

Why do you want to be a ...?

The wrong answer is to say you just want any job. Even for one paying the minimum wage you still need to be able to say why you are interested in that particular job. You could say that it is a part-time job and fits in around your studies, or that your mum was one and you have always been interested in this type of work. Whatever your reasoning, make it sound realistic.

What are your strengths? What is your biggest weakness?

We covered this in the previous chapter, so re-read your notes. Interviewers know people will have prepared answers to these questions so may ask them in a slightly different way, such as, 'What would your colleagues say if we asked them about your faults?' It can be best to discuss how you are working to overcome a weakness such as, 'I knew my business knowledge was weak, so I studied for a business studies diploma to improve my knowledge'.

Or you could describe how you turned a negative into a positive: 'My biggest weakness is that sometimes I work too hard, so my life can get out of balance', or 'My colleagues have told me that I can be too focused on my work and I have to remind myself to lighten up.'

You might like to present your strengths modestly with phrases such as, 'At my last appraisal my manager commented that...' or 'I was asking a client for some feedback the other day and they were kind enough to say...'

You can also present your weaknesses positively. For example, 'I can get impatient with people who put up obstacles so I've learned to listen more carefully.' A good technique is to describe an example from the past so you describe the weakness (such as finding it difficult to delegate in your first management role) and then how you overcame it.

Why should I hire you over the other people I have interviewed?

The interviewer expects you to be confident in answering this question so be assertive and proud of your efforts. This is another opportunity to remind the interviewer of your strengths.

Why did you choose your degree?

It's unlikely that you will be asked this unless you have recently left education, including following part-time study as a mature student. You do not want to say it was the only degree offered to you via clearing, or that your parents thought it was a good idea. Be confident in your explanation and what you gained from it.

What are your short and long-term goals?

Link this to the job you are applying for, so if you want to be a solicitor then a job as a legal executive is a step along the way, but it might seem odd to be applying for a job as an accounts clerk when you want to work as a make-up artist. Although you could say that in the longer term you would like your own business and this would provide useful background. The company will want to see you as someone likely to stay there for a couple of years, not just for six months as a stop gap.

Why are you looking to leave your current job? Or why are you contemplating leaving your company?

It may be because you have outgrown your previous job or are looking for a new challenge. Avoid saying anything detrimental about your boss or company, as you don't want them wondering what it is about you that is so difficult.

In a recession, companies expect some of their applicants to be unemployed but you can make this sound a bit more upbeat such as, 'I managed to survive two rounds of redundancy, but by the third round an additional 20% of people were let go, including me'.

What major problems did you encounter in your last job?

We all have challenges, and not everyone sees these as problems. Interviewers want people who have solved problems so think of one or two you could use as an example, and which were successfully resolved.

You don't have any experience of ... do you?

I always think this is an odd question to ask a candidate; if it was a problem you wouldn't have been shortlisted. Never say 'No, I don't.' Instead, talk about how you want to broaden your experience, how you are adaptable and quick to learn, etc, and also what you are able to bring to the job that other candidates may not be able to.

Why did you stay so long with one company?

Some interviewers expect people to move companies every three or so years to widen their experience, but if you were getting plenty of opportunities to develop yourself in the company why would you move?

You seem to have done a lot of job hopping. Why?

Some people have had quite a number of jobs. Sometimes this is in order to gain more experience to help them 'climb the ladder', whilst with other people it is because they were on short-term contracts. You could say that you are now seeking to develop your career in one company.

If you could choose any job what would it be? What is your ideal job?

This is not the time to fantasise about being a rock star, TV personality or dress designer. Your ideal job is this one that you have applied for.

What would you describe as your greatest achievement?

You probably have plenty of examples, but best to choose one that relates to the job, although not necessarily a work-based example. This could include gaining a good degree despite the serious illness of a close relative, or taking on a personal challenge.

What was your greatest challenge and how did you overcome it?

This would generally be a work-related answer but if you have climbed to the top of Ben Nevis, or some other physical challenge, this is often well received by an interviewer. Do always make sure you have an answer to this as it's another one that could be asked as a competency-based question. Think STAR!

Are you ambitious?

You could answer yes or no, but with these sorts of questions do follow up with more detail. You also need to be mindful of the job. Will it give scope for your ambition? Come across as too ambitious and the interviewer will be concerned that you will leave too soon. It might be better, in some circumstances, to emphasise the importance of job satisfaction.

Are you applying for other jobs?

Of course you are – you can't just apply for one job at a time. Let them know you are in discussions with other companies. They will be reassured that other companies are interested in you, but do emphasise your interest in their job.

What was the main weakness of your last boss?

It is surprising how many candidates will make negative comments. Don't be tempted to do the same. You could say that you have nothing but admiration for the way your boss works and in the past he has both challenged and supported you, but you have now outgrown the job or decided you want to refocus your career into a new area, hence applying for this job.

How would you describe your management style?

This question may well be asked if you are applying for a job as a manager or supervisor, so how would you describe your style? Some people have never verbalised this so it can be useful to think about it and be able to describe it. Sometimes it can be helpful to have read through a few management books to understand about different styles and so be clearer why you do what you do.

How do you prioritise when you are given too many tasks to accomplish?

This question could easily be asked as a competency question – can you give me an example of how you have prioritised when you have too many tasks to accomplish? Using the STAR approach could be very helpful in the way you structure your answer. You want to show how you will manage your time by differentiating between what is important and what is urgent.

Can you give me an example of teamwork and leadership?

This is a bit confusing; which do they want, an answer about teamwork or an answer about leadership? So when you answer, you need to make sure you cover both.

Do you prefer working on your own or in a team?

This is a closed question – you could just say 'in a team', so you need to open up and give more detail. If you know that the job is predominately one or the other then you could say that, for example, your preference is for teamwork, but you are still able and happy to work on your own as needed for the job.

Give me an example of when your work has been criticised. How did you respond?

When you answer this, make sure you describe an idea that was criticised, not your work, and you can show how you listened and took account of the feedback. For example, perhaps you wrote a business report, gave it to your boss but she returned it with some negative comments. You read through these comments carefully, reviewed your work and came back with a second version which was better received.

What do you see as your greatest strengths as an employee?

You already know your strengths, so refer to those, making sure they link in with what the new employer will want.

What would be the area you feel least confident about if we offered you the job?

Do not raise any concerns. You are being asked this to see if you are self-confident. Remind them of your strengths, how much you are looking forward to the job, and also how quick you are to learn.

How would your colleagues answer if we asked them about your faults?

As already mentioned, this is another way of getting you to describe your weaknesses. By asking the question this way, rather than asking you what you think, some interviewers will hope you let you guard down and are more open.

How would your last boss describe you?

This is another question to allow you to describe your strengths. Think of something specific such as, 'My boss told me I was a great team player, willing to get involved and someone the team could rely on.'

Where do you see yourself in five years time?

The company wants to know that you plan to stay for a while so stress your strengths and how you can use them in this job. You could say that you would like to grow your career with this company.

What are your interests?

Interviewers are always interested in unusual hobbies, but think about the transferable skills gained. For example, if you are an historical re-enactor you may have delivered a significant number of addresses at a living history camp, which would be of benefit to any job involving public speaking. It can often be helpful to have three different interests; one solitary, one team-based and perhaps one that is creative. If you are into a lot of sports or risky hobbies it's best not to mention them all or there may be concerns that you will be taking excessive sick leave due to illnesses caused by your skydiving, white-water rafting, and rugby playing.

Aren't you overqualified for this position?

There may be different and valid reasons why you are applying for a lower-level job; you may want a less stressful job because of personal commitments, you might be seeking to develop into a new area and are thus having to take a step or two back, or you may find it hard to get a job on the same level as your previous one and would rather be doing something than be out of work. Remind the interviewer of your strengths and how you can help them and their business.

Would you accept this job if I offered it to you?

Don't hesitate, say yes! You can save the negotiations for later.

Are you considering other jobs at this time?

Just say yes, and leave it at that.

How does this opportunity compare?

From what I've heard so far, it compares favourably and I'd like to know more.

 Are there any questions you are afraid of being asked? If so you need to write these down and practise them!

Handling the salary question

At interview you are likely to be asked questions relating to salary, basically how much you want, how much you get in your current job, if we offer you x will you take it, etc. When there are many people applying for every job, and some people are willing to take a pay cut you may feel a bit uneasy about negotiating the best deal possible, but if you know you are worth it, and have marketed yourself well through your application and performance at the assessment centre, then there are possibilities. When I worked with Lindsay, she had been earning £40,000 and after redundancy applied for a job that really interested her but she didn't think would pay as much. So we had a plan to negotiate – offer to work a four-day week for the money on offer (£32k). She took this approach and it worked, giving her one day a week to do consultancy, but this time could also be used to develop a hobby or for part-time study.

What salary are you seeking?

You don't want to be too specific at the interview stage, it's better to wait and negotiate once you get the job offer. Your initial research should have identified a typical range for the job, so reply with a question such as:

- How much does the job pay?
- I am much more interested in doing (type of work) for (organisation's name) than I am in the size of the initial offer.
- This company pays a fair salary, doesn't it?

Summarise the requirements of the position as you understand them and then ask the interviewer for the normal salary range at the company for that type of position.

How much are you earning in your current position?

The interviewer usually seeks to cap any salary ambitions, and most won't offer more than 10% above what you currently earn. If you know that your salary is low for the work that you do, be ready to explain any reasons for this and why it shouldn't guide current discussions.

Tell the interviewer that you would prefer learning more about the current position before you discuss compensation, and that you are confident you will be able to reach a mutual agreement about salary at that time.

The salary range for this position is £XX,000 to £YY,000, is that what you were expecting?

Tell the interviewer that it comes near what you were expecting, and then offer a range which places the top of the employer's range at the bottom of your range, i.e., 'I was thinking in terms of £YY,000 to £ZZ,000.' This **should** be consistent with what you have learned about the market rate for that position.

The salary is £X000 per month

Try not to look excited or disappointed. Simply repeat the salary, look up as though you were thinking about it, and pause. Don't worry about the silence. Give the employer an opportunity to increase the offer. If the interviewer does not change the offer, try the response suggested above.

What would be your reaction if we offered you the job but at £XX,000 p.a.? [Less than you hoped for]

You need to be realistic about your options, and balance a drop in salary with having a regular income. It may be best to say that you would be very willing to discuss this once they are sure that you are the best person for the job.

A practice interview

Many people will pay to have an interview-coaching session, and getting specific feedback can be incredibly beneficial, but it could be an expense you can't afford. The next best option is to have someone take you through a mock interview. Pass them this book, and ask them to ask you the questions. It can help to record the 'interview' as you can then play it back – did you sound enthusiastic and positive, were your answers clear? Then review your answers and think about how you could improve.

This will help you to get ready, but also be aware that you might be asked some unusual questions such as, 'If you were an animal, what sort of animal would you be?' It can be hard to know how best to respond. A panda might be considered too soft, a lion too aggressive, a snake … I think I'd like to be a zebra!

Rehearse but don't memorise

Practising answers will help you to feel better prepared, but you must make sure you don't come across as someone trying to remember a script. You are not memorising answers but having examples ready that you can call on.

Chapter 17. Over to you – questions to ask at the end of the interview

Why you need to ask questions

When you apply for a job you don't just send a CV but also a covering letter, and use it to enhance your application. In the same way, when you go for an interview you don't just answer the questions asked but also ask questions yourself. It enhances the impression you give.

The main part of the interview is lead by the interviewer. They ask the questions to hear what you have to say. It is then the 'over to you' stage where you get a chance to ask them some questions.

To stand out from the other candidates you should prepare questions to show that you have done your research and are interested in the company.

Don't be a candidate who says, 'everything has been covered'. Demonstrate you have thought about this job and ask some relevant questions.

How to develop questions

You could of course risk it, but better to do your preparation and demonstrate some thought behind the questions asked.

It can be helpful to consider questions from different categories, and they can cover:

- Questions related to the company

- Questions about the actual job

- Questions to show your enthusiasm

- Questions to emphasise your strengths

- And questions to imagine you in the role

You may have already got the answers to some of these questions during the interview so there's no need to ask again, and doing so might suggest that you weren't listening, but by creating a list of around five to seven you should have three or left to ask.

Questions related to the company

These can cover things you have found out from the company website, literature and through searching online. You may have already been asked a question by the interviewer about what you know but you could also ask a question to demonstrate the research you have done. Rather than a general question, link it to something you have read. For example:

I read on your website that you have recently launched a new range of beauty products in addition to your medical equipment. I'm interested in why the company did this.

Questions about the actual job

If it hasn't been covered in sufficient detail you can ask what you would be doing and how the vacancy has come up, who would be your manager and who you would be working with. Asking why the vacancy arose means you will know if this is a new position, or if you are replacing someone. You might like to find out whether they were promoted or left. Example questions include:

- *Can you tell me a bit more about the job role?*
- *Since the job was advertised, have your requirements been amended?*
- *How does this job contribute to the success, efficiency and profitability of the organisation?*
- *If I were to join the company, where might you see me in three to five years time?*

What would you see as my priorities in this job?

Questions to show your enthusiasm

Choose a question that shows your interest and enthusiasm, demonstrate what you really love about their products or company and ask to be shown around, if appropriate. You might also like to ask if there is any opportunity to study for relevant qualifications. Key questions:

Could I have a look around before I leave?

This shows enthusiasm and even if they say no, nothing has been lost.

If I am successful, can you tell me what happens in the first week?

This will help you find out if there is a structured induction plan or if you are going to be left to get on with it.

If I was to be offered the job, what preparation could I undertake?

This demonstrates your enthusiasm, interest and helps them to visualise you in the role.

Questions to emphasise your strengths

You could use some of these questions to bring in your background and previous experience. You may have some really great personal qualities and abilities but the questions asked haven't given you a chance to discuss these as yet. So have questions ready to bring out something in your background that you haven't been able to get across.

For example, if you are strong in problem-solving you could ask a question like:

Is there a need to solve problems in the job? I'm asking because this is one of my strengths and I've … [where you give a specific example.]

If you're an idea person, say:

Do you encourage staff to come up with new ideas? The reason I'm asking is...

TASK

Prepare a relevant question for each of your strengths. You can then ask a question that will enable you to emphasise a particular strength.

Imagining you in the role

I am very interested in this job and believe I can do it well; what concerns do you have about me as a candidate?

This question might encourage the interviewer to see you as successful in the role and as they imagine you, this just might increase your chance of getting the job. The interviewer may not like to commit themselves, but if they do, offer reassurance. It also demonstrates that you are receptive to feedback. For example, if they were to say, 'we were looking for someone with more direct experience', you can emphasise your transferable skills.

Many interviewers will not be comfortable answering this question so don't push it, but sometimes it can work!

Imagine that I excel in this position. Is there room for progression?

Better to ask now then to find out later there are no real prospects. But things can change. Years ago, when I applied for a job as a Post Office counter clerk, I was told there would be no opportunities for promotion; but a move to a regional centre resulted in me being promoted to a junior management position in less than a year.

Don't think you have to remember all of these questions; it's absolutely fine to have them written on a pad which you can refer to when the interview moves into this phase.

Even in the worst-case scenario when all your questions have already been covered, as you pull out your pad to check, the interviewer will see that you had thought about this and listed them down. You can say that everything has been covered.

What not to ask

There is a difference between what you want to know and the questions you should ask. Of course you want to know how much you will get paid, what your holiday entitlements are and if there are any perks to working for the company (discounts off goods, etc) but if you ask questions that relate to these areas the focus is on what you want to gain rather than telling them even more good things about how perfect you are for the job.

Once you get the job offer you can then find out the answers to these basic details about the terms and conditions.

A great finale to the interview

Once you have asked three or four questions you can thank the interviewer for answering your questions, tell them how much you are interested in the company and its products or services and that you are very interested in the job. You can either ask:

What are the next steps?

or the more detailed:

I'm really impressed with your company, its products/services and everyone that I have had the opportunity to meet. I'm confident I could do a great job in the position we've discussed. When can I expect to hear from you?

Try to get a specific time period to enable you to follow up if you haven't heard anything.

Alternatively you could deliver a closing statement.

Closing statements

This is where you summarise your qualifications for the position, your top skills, experience, and accomplishments so the interviewer is really clear on why they should hire you.

It must be short and to the point (60 seconds is the absolute maximum). You must know the top five reasons why you will be a great candidate and be able to weave these into the discussion.

If the selection is purely based on an interview you can thank the interviewer, and ask about the next step or stage. However, if the interview is part of an assessment centre this is unlikely to be the last element of the day, so get yourself ready for the next exercise.

During the interview you might have realised that this job is not a great fit, and you wouldn't accept it even if offered. You still, however, want to leave having made a good impression as a more suitable vacancy might arise at a later date.

Finally, don't forget to say goodbye to the receptionist or secretary as you leave.

On the Day and Following Up

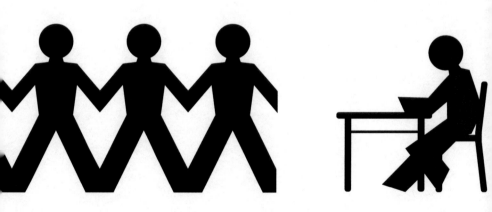

Chapter 18. Appearance and body language

You never get a second chance to make a first impression

Alongside preparing for the interview and assessment centre activities, you also need to consider your appearance and body language.

Appearance

At assessment centre and interview you are being assessed formally, and judgements are also being made on how you look and behave. The assessors will expect to see somebody who fits in with the other people working in the company. So for a job in the City this is likely to mean a dark suit and a plain-coloured shirt, high fashion for a job in the fashion industry, and perhaps something which makes a strong statement for some creative industries. We all have our own style, whether it is consciously or unconsciously created, and you want this to be accepted rather than to shock. If you choose to wear the clothes you wear for a night out it might be ok, but it might shock an interviewer who finds it distracting and difficult to put their initial reactions to one side. Even I was surprised to interview someone in punk bondage clothes (a while ago) for a graduate entrant position, and I did wonder if they had worn the clothes for a dare.

The clothes you wear should be appropriate to the job and organisation. It's when you look out of place that people notice, but you also want to wear clothes that make you feel good, and that will increase your confidence levels.

To be well-dressed you must wear clothes that complement you physically and are appropriate for the occasion. For some jobs it will help to be stylishly dressed, for others a more conservative style is appropriate. If in doubt aim to dress on the smarter side and wear clothes to suit the company culture. An open neck shirt and chinos may be suitable for some companies, but if in doubt, opt for a suit. It is unlikely that you will ever look too smart, although if you are going for a more manual job you will be better in smart casual dress than overly formal.

Naturally your clothes should be clean and well pressed, although not all candidates dress this way.

If you can find out in advance how people within the organisation typically dress, you can put together the right look. Try on your interview outfit and think about how accessories, your hair, and general physical grooming will contribute to the effect. Work on this as carefully as you worked on your CV. People do make initial judgements and you want others to have a positive one of you.

I once interviewed someone for a senior-level job in a charity, whose application was supported by very well-known TV presenters, but he arrived for interview looking like he'd come straight off the allotment. He didn't look like he cared and maybe he had thought the interview was a formality, but it wasn't.

If in doubt about what suits you a session with an image consultant might prove money well spent.

You must try on your clothes in advance to make sure that they are comfortable, and they won't crease too much. If you have put on some weight, don't squeeze into clothes which are too tight, as it is hard to concentrate when your waistband cuts in.

As you get ready you need to ensure that your clothes will stay clean and you cover contingencies in case of accidents, e.g. a spare pair of tights or tie. Make sure your shoes are clean and polished, your glasses are clean and free of dust and also consider jewellery. By all means wear your wedding and engagement rings, but don't wear too many rings. For men, a wedding ring or signet ring is enough. Some interviewers don't like to see earrings on men and remove any other piercing unless you are confident it's acceptable. Make sure your wristwatch is in keeping with your overall appearance and your watch face and strap are clean. Also take a handkerchief, a pen and pad and a hairbrush or comb to avoid the windswept look.

Avoid wearing too much perfume or aftershave. This is not a date! While you may think you smell wonderful, your particular fragrance may be overpowering to the interviewer. Wear discreet make-up; do not over-apply lipstick, blusher, eye make-up or powder. Do make sure your hands and nails are clean. If you have chipped nail polish or bite your nails, remove the polish.

If you smoke, or live with someone who does, make sure your clothes don't smell of smoke. Give them a good airing. If you must smoke beforehand, make sure you have some mints with you. The odour of cigarette smoke is offensive to most non-smokers.

The importance of body language

Body language is important. It can help to build relationships with others and can be used to good effect at both interview and in the assessment centre exercises.

Eye contact

We expect people to look at us, and people appear shifty if they don't; we also wonder if they are interested in us. You can try an experiment. Tell a friend that you are going to have a discussion for three minutes and they need to avoid eye contact. You'll find it hard to concentrate. So when other people talk to you, whether it be the interviewer or someone in the group exercise, do look at them as they talk; certainly in any assessed exercise it will go in your favour and you will get some positive points towards a competence such as 'building relationships'.

You don't need to stare, and it is fine to look away, especially when you are thinking of what to say, but do return your focus to the other person or people.

 If you feel uncomfortable holding eye contact with people, look at their forehead, just above their nose.

Gestures

Some gestures can be helpful, such as the way we use our hands when we are talking and perhaps raising an eyebrow if something is interesting, but we don't want to do too much or it is distracting. When some people are nervous they fidget, such as tapping the desk, playing with their hair, or twirling a pen. Done occasionally these are fine, but done too much and other people can get distracted. I've found it off-putting when interviewing someone who kept clicking a pen on and off, as it made it more difficult for me to concentrate.

> You can smile! You don't need to be serious all of the time and this demonstrates some warmth to the other people you meet.

Voice tone

Some people sound boring, there is no variety in how they speak and it can lead to others not paying attention. It can help to have a friendly tone of voice, but don't be overly cheerful, and use some variations in pitch and speed, with emphasis on what is key, especially when presenting.

Do make sure that others can hear you, especially in a group session. You mustn't talk too softly or your comments might be missed, especially by the assessors. It is also important to convey enthusiasm in your voice so don't just say that you enjoy helping customers with problems, but use an enthusiastic rather than a flat tone.

If you have had quite a few interviews you may find that you have answered the same question over and over again, but make sure you still sound fresh, despite having to regularly repeat it. You have to sound enthusiastic and make your answer sound like it is the first time you have said it.

How you talk

In an interview situation – often thought a stressful experience, our voice may often change from a normal tone to perhaps something high pitched or else we stumble and get our words confused. This is when practice can really help. The more you practise answering interview questions out loud the more your voice is likely to sound confident.

There is also a tendency for people to rush though their answer – often talking so fast that the interviewer can't grasp what they have to say – so take your time and speak more slowly, putting emphasis on certain words.

We can often have a tendency to say 'umm' and 'you know' and other such phrases. We are often not aware of doing this and sometimes when my husband listens to me on the phone he points out that I add 'errs' into my sentences when I'm thinking, so be conscious of it and try to cut out some of these.

Posture

People will notice your posture when you are stood up, walking and sat down. As you enter a room, walk in with your head held high and look confident.

Some people, and not just younger candidates, slouch in their chair. This suggests laziness and a lack of interest, so practise sitting more upright with both feet on the floor. You can also lean forward slightly as that demonstrates interest in what the other person is saying.

Avoid the temptation to lean on the interviewer's desk, as they are likely to see you as invading their personal space and that won't help to develop a rapport. Also avoid having your arms crossed in front of your body; it might feel comfortable to you, but to others it looks defensive.

Chapter 19. On the day

This is an important day. You will have spent hours on your application, research and final preparation and the purpose of all of this is to get you the job, so this is going to be your chance to demonstrate just how perfect you are for it.

You will want to answer questions to the best of your ability and revising what you prepared in earlier chapters will help, but you should also make sure that you follow these points:

- In some ways it is like preparing for a race. You need to be well prepared, you want some adrenaline flowing but you also need to stay calm and focused.

- Make sure you get a good night's sleep and if you have been doing preparation work, practising tests, and reading materials, stop and give your brain a rest.

- Begin the day with breakfast and take a snack with you. A slow energy-release breakfast (porridge or boiled eggs) should keep the hunger pangs away till lunchtime and if you need to leave early perhaps take a banana or an energy bar, which is far better than a sugary snack.

- Be mindful of lunch too! I was once an assessor at an assessment centre which started at 12.00 and no food was provided. The poor candidates had to manage on biscuits and coffee. When I was a candidate for a job with a well-known consultancy firm I found myself almost pushed out of the door at lunchtime and told to come back an hour later. I'd no idea where I was (strange city), it was raining and I hadn't got a brolly. I decided I didn't want to work for them anyway!

- Check your interview clothes a few days in advance, just in case there are minor repairs needed or a trip to the dry cleaners is in order. Dress as you would for the job; a suit for most office-based jobs is appropriate but smart casual is fine for, say, an interview as an electrician. You don't want to arrive at the interview looking smarter than the boss.

- Pack your briefcase the night before and take all relevant paperwork, spare copies of your CV, a notebook with your list of questions, a good quality pen (not a cheap ballpoint) and something to read in case you are kept waiting. Don't forget to take a watch and also some highlighter pens. If possible taking a spare pair of tights (women) and tie (men) can be useful in case of accidents.

- If you chew gum, remove it before you get out of the car, suck a mint to make sure your breath is fresh and if your hands get clammy, use an antiperspirant spray.

- You have to be ready and on time for the interview or assessment centre, so make sure you know where you are going, you have change for the meter or have arranged onsite parking, and allow time in case of delays.

- Alongside knowing where you are going, make sure you have the name of the person you are to meet when you arrive. Also have all the contact numbers on you, just in case of any problems during the journey.

- Ideally you will arrive about 10 minutes early. Too far in advance and they won't be ready for you, but you don't want to be cutting it fine. Be friendly with the people you meet as sometimes receptionists are asked informally about the candidates.

- The people you will meet at the assessment centre will be the assessors, centre manager and possibly a test administrator. The centre manager should greet you when you arrive, make you feel welcome and talk you through what will happen over the day.

You may arrive for your interview/assessment centre with a coat, umbrella, briefcase and more. See if you can leave some of these items at reception or in the cloakroom so you don't have to carry them around with you, and don't necessarily accept a drink when you arrive, otherwise you may

> You know you should switch your phone off, but regularly phones still ring at interview. More than once I've had a candidate take the call. They may apologise but it doesn't make a good impression.

have to juggle a cup of coffee alongside trying to shake hands when you are greeted by your interviewer or assessment centre manager.

It can be useful to visit the toilet if the interview or assessment centre is at the place you would work, to get a bit of a feel for the environment. You can also check that your hair is tidy and you don't have anything stuck in your teeth!

Be in a positive frame of mind

You may or may not feel confident but whilst you are being interviewed or assessed you must portray a positive image. There's some research that says smiling can help make you feel happy. So put a smile on your face and keep your eyes smiling as well.

Deal with the stress

It's natural to feel a bit tense and anxious, but use this to your advantage, like an actor before going on stage. It will make you more alert.

Everyone feels nervous before an interview and butterflies in your stomach are caused by the same surge of adrenaline that an athlete gets before an important race. It's the body's way of tuning up your faculties for peak performance. You can use this energy by keeping super-alert and noticing the interviewer(s) body language for clues on how much detail you should be giving them. For example, are they attentive or bored?

There are things you can do to help you to calm down and one of the best ways to help is to regulate your breathing. Breathe in through your nose and exhale quietly through your mouth. This helps you to relax. Practise such breathing in advance of the interview situation.

Breathing

When we are nervous we tend to breathe shallower, so we take in air but all the breathing is done at the top of our chest, not deep in our diaphragm. When we notice this happening we need to breathe slowly and deeply. Not only does it get more oxygen through to our brain but it also means that we feel less nervous.

I always recommend to my clients that they focus on their breathing and consciously count in for 4, hold for 8 and out for 16 as they walk to the interview and at any other time that they feel nervous. Why not try it now? Slowly breathe in through your nose and out through your mouth. Doing it a few times can really help.

If you have done all the preparation I've suggested this should help you, but also keep the interview in perspective. If you don't get the job you will still have learned a lot, which should help you to improve for next time. Your post-assessment centre or interview feedback will help, too.

Some people don't seem stressed at all, and perhaps they should do. *Never* think that an interview is a formality, and that you just need to turn up. It doesn't matter who you have on your side, you still need to perform well on the day.

During the day drink plenty of water to keep you hydrated and don't overdo the caffeine – you might get a buzz to begin with but it can add to your anxiety levels and increase the need for comfort breaks.

Be confident in your performance

People spend time practising interview questions and making sure they have interview clothes that make them look and feel good, but as well as these external things you also need to look inside and make sure your 'inner voice' has confidence in your ability. If you hear your inner voice say things like, 'I probably won't get this, other people will be more qualified than me, I hate group discussions, I find it hard to make an impact...' then it's not going to help you be successful.

These thoughts are likely to raise your anxiety level. You may find it better if you tell yourself:

- This is going to be a really interesting interview.
- I'm looking forward to talking about my experience with XYZ.
- I want to learn more about the company.
- I will be fine whether I get the job or not.

This will help you be calmer and enable you to focus on your strengths. It can be easy for negative thoughts like these to come into your head during the interview:

- I'm too old or young for the job.
- I rambled through that answer.
- What if I don't get the job?

But this distracts you from doing your best, so as these thoughts come into your head, ignore them! Take deep breaths and stay calm.

Be confident and expect to do your best. Remind yourself of times you have done really well in the past.

Do a mental rehearsal, remembering the last successful interview you had. What did it feel like, what did you see? Capture only the positive feelings as this will help you to feel more confident if you carry your positive attitude to interview. (NLP practitioners will anchor this by getting you to squeeze two fingers together as you remember these positive thoughts and feelings. In the interview, squeezing these two fingers again will recapture those positive thoughts and feelings.)

It will help to have a list of your strengths and positive qualities. Read the list to remind you of your greatest qualities and accomplishments. Read this just before you go into the interview and then put your notes carefully away.

When you arrive at the assessment centre

Make sure you are on time and have the name of the person you are to meet handy. All candidates will wait in the reception area or main assessment room and you might want to make some small talk with the others. If there is going to be a group exercise it often helps to have already got to know your fellow candidates.

There may be some paperwork to complete and as a group you will be told the structure of the day and given your own individual timetable. Most assessment centres include a group discussion and it is here where you are likely to have to provide a short introduction about yourself.

Introductions

Early on in the assessment centre you are likely to have to introduce yourself to the other participants. I've been nervous in the past and got a bit tongue-tied, so I learnt a technique to help; prepare in advance and make a note of what the introduction should cover on your timetable or a piece of paper so you can subtly refer to it. You might not be asked exactly what you have prepared but an introduction should cover:

- Your name

- Where you are from – university or current company

- What you are currently doing – the course you are studying, some brief details on your job

- Something interesting about you – perhaps related to a hobby

Listen carefully and make a note of what you are asked, so that you answer the right questions.

This is your chance to make a good first impression and by practising you shouldn't come across too nervous. Generally, introductions are done sat around the table but be aware that there is always a possibility that you have to stand at the front; if so this is more like a presentation, so read Chapter 12. The assessors will also introduce themselves.

First impressions count

We all know that people form opinions about each other within seconds of meeting so we need to create a great first impression. Some of this will be down to what you look like, voice tone and mannerisms, and also how you greet the interviewer and your response to the first question, so plan ahead to ensure that the first impression is favourable. This is known as the 'halo effect'. The opposite is the 'horns effect', when a bad start such as the way you are dressed, or spilling a cup of tea into your lap, makes it an uphill struggle to overturn this initial opinion.

Be natural and self-assured, but not overconfident or overbearing. Demonstrate some passion for the job, as interviewers warm to candidates who do this, and if you aren't passionate now when you want the job they will think you are unlikely to demonstrate any once you have been in the job for a while.

Interviewers want candidates who are confident and enthusiastic for the job. If you are only applying for it because you think you have to and are not very interested in it then you are unlikely to show enthusiasm. You don't demonstrate interest and enthusiasm solely by what you say but also by how you say it. However well thought through your answers to questions, most interviewers will make a final decision based on your enthusiasm and keenness to do the job. Of course you need to have answered the questions well, but when a decision is between two candidates, it is the one who has demonstrated enthusiasm and keenness that is most likely to get the job. This is not just enthusiasm without any substance; it is based on knowing who you are and why you want the job.

For the majority of the interview you will be answering questions and will use all the preparation you did in the previous chapter. Make sure you read it again and also do a practice interview.

If things go wrong

Things might go wrong, so here are some suggestions for how to deal with certain situations:

- **You arrive late:** As soon as you know you are going to be late, let the company know so they can look to rearrange if possible. For some jobs there will not be another chance to attend an assessment centre so you need to allow for contingencies. If in doubt it is best to stay in a nearby hotel the night before.

- **Punctuality.** Alongside arriving on time, you must also ensure you are ready for each exercise and meeting. Too many candidates go missing or arrive for each meeting late. This plays havoc with a timetable and does not endear you to the assessors or interviewers, so make sure you are ready a few minutes in advance.

- **If you get some bad news on the day.** Getting upset in an interview, whatever the cause, will be very bad for your chances. If you feel under par, you could drop a line afterwards explaining what happened. But the best solution may be to ring beforehand, explain the situation over the phone and see if another appointment can be found, or at least request that your particular circumstances are taken into account.

An assessment centre will combine a number of exercises so refer to the relevant chapters to ensure that you are clear about what to expect and follow the hints and tips. One of the most important things to remember is to **read all the instructions carefully and do exactly what they ask.** A highlighter pen can be helpful to **highlight the key detail.** We've already covered preparing for interviews and how to answer questions, let's now look at how to do your best at interview.

The interview

Introduction

An effective interviewer will put you at ease and let you know what is going to happen. This is all part of the introduction; they will either collect you and take you to the interview room or stand up as you knock at the door and ask you to sit down. If they proffer their hand, then shake it and make sure you are neither a limp fish nor a bone-crasher. If your hands are prone to sweating, some antiperspirant can help.

A typical introduction will have the interviewer tell you their name and job title, how long the interview will last and how the interview will be structured. For example, four competences will be covered and 10 minutes allocated to each. There will be time to ask any questions at the end. You will also be asked to help yourself to water, and whether you mind that they take notes. They will often say that if any question is unclear you ought not to hesitate in asking for clarification.

You should expect to get on well with the interviewer and look to develop a rapport; people want to appoint those who are easy to get on with. Occasionally it can be hard to develop a rapport with someone. Don't let it put you off if you really want the job. Try to 'like' them as much as possible during the interview because feelings such as these can communicate themselves through your body language. After the interview, you may like to reflect whether you want to join the company, particularly if you will be working closely with the interviewer.

The body of the interview

You may well get the classic first question – tell me a bit about yourself – to put you at ease, and then move into the competency-based questions. You will answer using the STAR system (see Chapter 16).

Your replies

Speak clearly and loud enough to be heard – you don't want your interviewer having to struggle to hear you – and make sure your voice sounds interesting, not monotone.

Don't feel that you need to answer immediately; you can always take a few seconds to collect your thoughts and if you aren't clear on the question it is better to ask for it to be repeated than to answer the wrong one. If you have a technical specialism you may not be interviewed by someone with your level of technical knowledge so make sure you can explain things in simpler terms. As you respond make sure that you are really answering the question and not rambling.

Sometimes when we are asked a question our mind goes blank. This usually occurs when people are extremely nervous. If it happens to you take a couple of deep breaths (which will calm you down by getting oxygen to your brain) and try to get your perspective again. If nervous, you can stall for time by saying something like, 'I couldn't quite hear you, could you repeat that please?' Or you could tell the truth and say, 'I'm sorry, my mind has gone blank.' You could then explain that you are prone to nerves in interviews and your honesty may save the day (unless you are applying for a job that requires you to keep your nerve, such as a fire-fighter).

Your preparation will have identified why you are suitable for the job and, as you answer questions, mentally tick off the ones that have been covered – then at the end you can always add something that you think would be relevant, such as by saying 'Would it be helpful if I mentioned something else relevant to this job?'

> Take every opportunity to explain your achievements and abilities within the context of the job description.

Questions you can't answer

Some interviewers will ask you questions that they know you can't answer. This is done to see how well you can deal with the unexpected, and often the answer is less relevant than the approach you take. If the question is a factual one and you don't know, then admit this with a smile and explain that this particular question is outside of your experience. If the question is a theoretical one, ask for a few moments to collect your thoughts so that you can give a considered answer. Preface any answer with, 'I'm not sure if this is exactly what you are asking, but...'

You may get asked questions on how you would deal with a situation. A good way of responding is to imagine yourself as a consultant and a client has brought this problem to you; how would you deal with it?

You may be asked questions on things that went wrong. It's fine to discuss mistakes, you don't need to hide them, but make sure to cover what you learnt from them. Admitting one or two mistakes can make you seem more real and give your positive examples greater credibility.

As the interview draws to a close, the interviewer will say something like 'That's all the questions I have for you, is there anything you would like to ask me?' That's your chance to ask some questions, and we covered this in Chapter 17.

They should then let you know the next steps, although in an assessment centre this is often dealt with by the assessment centre manager.

Chapter 20. Afterwards

After an interview you should take time to review how things went, and be ready for the follow-up.

Most people feel such a sense of relief that an assessment centre or interview is over that they just want to clear their head, relax and unwind and try to forget about it. But wait five or 10 minutes before you go into unwind mode and instead do a review of how it went.

Make notes on as much as you can remember, from the interviewer(s) name, to more detail on the job and if anything was mentioned about salary. Then review how you came across, what went well and how you could improve for next time.

Ask yourself:

Preparation

- How adequately did I prepare myself for the interview?
- Was there anything I should have known about the company that I did not?
- Was I fully prepared for the group exercise? What further preparation would have helped?
- Was I fully prepared for the written exercise? What further preparation would have helped?
- Was I fully prepared for the role-play? What further preparation would have helped?
- Was I fully prepared for the presentation? What further preparation would have helped?
- Was I fully prepared for the psychometric testing? What further preparation would have helped?

Body language

- Was I in the right frame of mind?
- Was my eye contact right?
- Did I smile?

Interview question-handling

- Which questions did I handle well?
- Which questions did I handle poorly?
- How thorough were my answers?
- How well did I emphasise how my skills would benefit this position?
- How well did I ask questions?
- What could I have done differently?
- Were there any questions I could not answer to my satisfaction?
- Did I give answers which didn't seem to satisfy the interviewer?
- Did I answer the questions in a way that stressed the most important aspects, my ability, my willingness and my suitability?
- Did I talk too much?
- Was I able to discuss my strengths and weaknesses?
- Did I say why I wanted to work for the organisation?
- Did I find out all I needed to?
- Did I ask some good questions at the end?

Relationship with the interviewer or assessor

- How effective was my performance in the interview/assessment centre?

- Was the interviewer interested and involved in what I was saying?

- Did I show that I was listening to the interviewer?

- Did the interview flow or was it stilted?

Personal qualities

- Having seen the people in the company, how appropriately was I dressed?

- Did I present an accurate and favourable picture of myself?

- Did I look my best?

- Was I relaxed and in control of myself?

- Did I appear confident and show genuine enthusiasm?

- Did I seem interested and enthusiastic about the job?

Other

- Would I like to work for that organisation?

- What additional research do I need to do before a subsequent interview?

- Where there any areas I could have prepared better?

- Do my answers still sound fresh, despite having to regularly repeat them?

Follow up with a thank-you letter

One of the very best ways to stand out from the rest is to send a thank-you letter. Typically, only about 25% of applicants write a letter to thank the interviewer or assessors for their time. If the company is still deciding between you and another applicant, this may just tip the balance in your favour.

It is worth spending the time to do this as it reinforces your strengths, and demonstrates your written communication skills. If your handwriting is good, then handwritten has more impact than typed, but speed of delivery is very important. If you can't get the letter there the next day, it's better to send it by email.

Your thank-you letter can reiterate your strengths and also cover any areas of weakness or possible concerns. You can say how your strengths can overcome any weaker areas. You should have addressed these in the interview but often it is only afterwards that we can recall an example, so get the letter written now.

Structure of a thank-you letter

Paragraph 1: Thank you for interviewing me for the position of xyz on (date).

Paragraph 2: Restate what you have to offer to the company.

After discussing the responsibilities of the job, I am sure that I have the skills and experience to perform well in this position.

Mention again what you can bring to the job.

Add in an extra paragraph here if you need to provide a more detailed answer to a particular question. For example:

During the interview you asked why I would be a good candidate and I could only give

you a vague response. I have spent a good
deal of time since then evaluating my
strengths in relation to your needs. After
serious consideration I can comfortably
state that I am a good candidate because …

Paragraph 3: Thank the interviewer. Say how you may be
contacted.

Thank you again for taking the time to meet
with me. If you need additional
information, I can be reached on xyz.

Julie told me that after she had started a new job, her
boss told her that he had been undecided between her
and another candidate, and it was receiving the thank
you letter which made the difference.

Waiting

It can sometimes feel like a long time has passed since your
interview or time at an assessment centre and you may wonder if
you will ever hear anything. However, the assessment process may
still be going on, particularly when several jobs are available, so
this can take several weeks and final decisions are not made until
everyone is able to get together for a review meeting.

If it is probable that the assessment process is over, a telephone
call asking about your status in the search is appropriate.

You get a regret letter

If you get a regret letter: 'We regret to inform you...' it could be for one of five reasons:

1. **There was not a good match between you and the job.** In this case, the rejection letter is a positive outcome. You would not have liked that job anyway.

2. **Your do not have the right background for this job.** You may not be ready for this job yet. If you applied, for example, to be a marketing manager, think of applying for a marketing executive job or gathering more experience.

3. **There was a good match but you simply did not interview well.** You need to spend time on interview practice.

4. **The applicant pool was extremely competitive:** There may have been more than one person who was capable of doing the job. The final decision may have been based on factors outside your control. The person who got the job may have been an internal candidate or had something extra to offer.

5. **There is no job available.** This could be because the head office wants to fill the vacancy but the local branch has no intention of filling it, or the job has already been offered to someone, and the advert was 'merely going through the motions'. Another possibility is that the job is being downsized and will go to someone the company intends to make redundant.

Whatever you think is the reason you didn't get the job, contact the company and ask for feedback.

Finally, even if you do not get an offer, you can still write one last letter. The person who has been offered the job may turn it down and this could lead to an offer for you. It will also leave a favourable impression.

Replying to the regret letter

There is no harm in sending one last (short) letter, certainly not to challenge their decision, but as another chance to create a good impression. You might have been a close second or third and this might mean you get contacted should the new employee not work out. So your reply could be something along the lines of:

Thank you for your phone call to tell me that the assistant manager vacancy has been filled. Although I was not selected for the position, I want to wish you and the new assistant manager well as you begin to work together. Once again, thank you for the consideration you have given my application for this position. Should there be a vacancy in the future, I hope you will keep me in mind and contact me.

In the meantime if you are able to give me some feedback on how I could improve my assessment centre performance for next time I would find it very helpful.

The letter asks for feedback on how you came across at the assessment centre and this should be helpful for future interviews. Not all companies will provide feedback and some will refuse to give feedback to anyone. However, it is well worth asking – so do make contact and don't be afraid to follow up if you don't hear anything.

You've got the job!

If you get a job offer, you will want to consider whether it is the right job for you, and then to negotiate the salary and benefits package, if available. Read again how to respond to salary questions as covered in Chapter 16.

Of course, you may decide to decline. If so, do it promptly and, within your letter, keep the possibility of you getting in touch again in the future.

Success

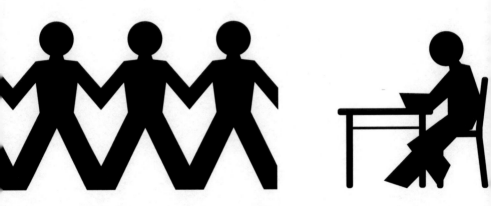

Chapter 21. You've got the job!

If you have got the job, well done! It's wonderful news to hear that you have been offered a job. You may be told there and then, right after your interview. You might get a phone call a day or so later, or the result may come by letter or email. Often the bigger the company, the longer they take to get back to you. Whether you are told face to face or by phone make sure that you **sound enthusiastic**, to reinforce that they made the right choice.

You may well have some questions to ask, and the company expect people to have specific questions. So you could say something like:

Thank you so much, I'm really thrilled. Can you let me know what happens next?

or:

Thank you so much. Can you give me more details on the job offer or will I receive something in writing in the next day or so?

They will probably tell you that you will get confirmation in writing including details on pay, holiday, etc.

You don't have to accept the job right away. Especially if you think another company may make you an offer or if you aren't 100% certain that you want the job. So it's fine to ask for a day or so to review the offer, and waiting to get it in writing will give you some extra time.

When you have made your decision, phone to accept and make sure to sound enthusiastic on the phone. Then confirm your acceptance in writing.

Of course, you may decide to turn an offer down. If so do it quickly and send a letter which keeps the possibility of you getting in touch again in the future. A typical letter is:

Thank you for offering me a position as a design consultant. I found our discussions during the interview process helpful in learn more about the details of this position. I appreciated the time you allowed me to consider your offer.

Throughout the interview process, my initial impressions of Company XYZ as an outstanding organisation were confirmed. However, after considerable thought about my career goals, I have chosen to accept the offer from an employer based closer to my home town.

I'm sorry to have to decline your job offer. This was a difficult decision, although I believe it is the right one for me.

I want to thank you for the time and consideration you have given my application. It was a pleasure meeting you and learning more about Company XYZ.

The first 90 days

It's fantastic to get a new job, and like most people you will want to make a great impression but you may also be a little apprehensive.

It's tempting to want to make an initial impact, but you should listen and learn. Your colleagues and team members won't be pleased to have you making changes right away.

Can you find out even more about the company?

In the period between getting the job offer and starting the job find out as much as you can about the company. Ask for or download a copy of the company's most recent annual report and read it thoroughly. Ask for materials about the company, such as information about its products and services and/or business strategies, anything that will allow you to gain a little extra knowledge. Jot down key questions you want to get answered.

Start with a clean sheet

In the same way you research the company, do an in-depth personal inventory of your own skills, behaviours and attitudes. Think about previous jobs and experiences: what worked for you, what didn't, and why. You've got an ideal opportunity to **build the new and improved professional you**. Write down the personal characteristics that you'd like to improve. Then, develop a strategy to maximise your strengths and minimise your weaknesses. For instance, if you were never prepared for meetings, write down ways to improve your performance. If you were always late on assignments, develop a routine that will keep you on time.

Don't expect everything to be perfect

You have asked so many questions. You think you know exactly how things will go, but then it doesn't proceed as planned. Expect this, and tell yourself to be relaxed and take things as they come. Understand that the reality of any situation rarely lives up to what was reported, or what your expectations were. Expect some things to be better than advertised, some worse, some the same. That way when you find out, for example, about the need to travel to meetings on a weekly basis or to take your turn at looking after your boss's child when she comes in after school, you will be better able to cope.

Expect there to be a crisis at home

It's Murphy's Law you will get toothache or the car will play up or you need to get the washing machine fixed on the day you are due to start your new job. What you can do is make sure the house is clean and you are up-to-date on the shopping and ironing and general chores a few days before you start.

Decide on the image you want to portray

We all have an image, whether created consciously or not. Before going in on the first day, consider what 'image' the employer feels is appropriate to your job – appearance, clothes, lifestyle, attitude, etc. It helps to fit in on the first day. Don't let your clothes attract more attention than your ideas. Think about your behaviour; what could be offensive? Drinking alcohol at lunchtime? Using swear words? Monitor your behaviour so you can see where you may want or need to change.

Be friendly

Make sure to say hello or good morning and smile to everyone when you arrive at work, but do not share too much personal information about your social life or how stressed you feel about the job.

Give your new colleagues the benefit of the doubt if you don't feel at ease with them right away. Think how long it takes for stepfamilies to get used to each other. The dynamics can be similar for a new worker. On one level, your new work team will welcome you. On another level, they may worry about how they will have to change because of you.

Don't be too keen on making a good impression

There is a lot to take in with a new job, so pace yourself. Remember that you are learning a new job, building relationships and settling into a new team. All of this will take time. The temptation might be to work like mad to prove yourself worthy of your new role, but you will do better if you take the time to reflect, refocus and reprioritise. You don't want to have to slow down at a later point. It may look like you have lost your enthusiasm.

Wait before making suggestions for change

You have lots of ideas to make a difference, and want to let the company know they made the right choice in recruiting you, but don't try to change things at once, seek to understand first. You want to make sure you show them how you can do the job and fit in. Before you start making changes, try to understand why things are done the way they are. It can then help when you do want to make a suggestion, as people will notice that you took the time to understand. Then don't try to make too many changes at once, choose a small achievable goal first.

Keep balance

Don't forget the other priorities in your life – your family, your health, your hobbies, your friends. If all facets of your life are not in alignment, there's no way you will find fulfilment in your job. Remember, you work to live not live to work.

Keep a notebook

Always carry a notepad or pocket organiser with you. Get into a routine of writing down thoughts, ideas, and information from others. Before you forget, buy one now!

Get to know your colleagues

Find out about their likes and dislikes. Let others know that you're interested in how they do things. Understand their work style. Don't form close relationships too quickly – someone perceived as a troublemaker may be very friendly but you don't want to be associated with them – instead concentrate on fitting in with everyone. For example, you can offer to make the coffee or take the post to the post room. Make sure you know how to use the office equipment and if a problem arises, such as a paper jam in the copier, try to fix it rather than leave it for others to sort out.

Your job

If you do not already have a job description, ask for one, and then try to define as clearly as you can the boundaries of your job. You are not seeking to establish the minimum acceptable benchmarks, but frontiers within which you can make your best contribution. Do this constructively and as soon as you can. The first month is ideal. Six months later is too late.

You also need to ask a lot of questions. This won't show any deficiency in you. Rather, you'll show that you can learn what you need to know. You can ask as many questions as you want at the beginning. Do help by grouping questions together and not asking one question every few minutes.

Understand the network of people

You need to view relationships across the organisation and beyond. Understand how to manage internal politics, recognise the key influencers, the gatekeepers, and the allies who will help you achieve your goals. Draw a hub-and-spoke diagram with you in the centre and identify the important relationships you need to cultivate.

Make sure you know the length and terms of your probation period. It's natural to feel anxious about this, but you don't have to wait until the end of the period to get feedback on your work. Set up some talks with your boss. Point out what you've accomplished so far. And ask about each area of your job. What is going well? What could be improved – and how?

Get motivated each day

Before you start work each day, get yourself motivated. Stop asking questions like, 'Why do I have to go to work?' and reframe by asking, 'What can I contribute today?'

At the end of each working day, review what you have done

Give yourself a pat on the back for what you have accomplished, and think about what you have learnt from things that didn't go so well.

Plan what you are going to do tomorrow, the night before

Either do this before you leave work or in the evening but do take the time to plan what you will do tomorrow. What is important and urgent? If you haven't done it the night before, do it first thing and follow the plan. Don't get sucked into spending, say, two hours on emails unless it's necessary.

It's always fantastic to get a job offer and just like you prepared for your application and the interview or assessment centre, this final chapter has given you a number of suggestions for how to prepare for the first few months in your new job. You will want to create a great first impression, so adopt or adapt suggestions accordingly. Remember though that none of us are perfect, and if things go wrong it is okay. Better to try and fail, than not try at all. The first few weeks are about adapting so don't be afraid to ask for advice.

You may like to keep a journal in order to review your progress so in three to six months time, when you really fit in and all is going smoothly, you can look back and evaluate/assess/reflect on the steps you took. It will be useful to refer to this for your next career move.

A Final Word

I've shared much of what I cover with my career coaching clients, so if you have carefully read and followed the advice in this book you should have greatly increased your chance of success.

Getting a job is sometimes out of our hands though, and there are equally good rival candidates out there. Many times I've agonised with my fellow assessors as to who gets the job offer. Sometimes we can be spoilt for choice.

As you apply for jobs do review your performance and be accurate and honest on how you did, learning so that you can improve for next time. You also need to keep your motivation up, and not take knock-backs too personally.

Sometimes people appreciate some one-to-one advice on a specific application or assessment centre, or want an interview-coaching session. If you would like to schedule time to work with me I'd be delighted to hear from you.

I also run an electronic newsletter ('How to get a job you love'), and have done for eight years, which is sent to your inbox at the start of each month. Do visit my website to sign up for it, and also visit my blog for regular articles and comments on career-related topics.

Wishing you every success,

Denise Taylor

www.amazingpeople.co.uk

www.twitter.com/amazingpeople

Answers to Psychometric Tests

Chapter 4. Verbal reasoning and critical thinking tests

Test 1 (Verbal reasoning)

1. Catalytic converters are most effective in reducing pollution when cars are used for short journeys.

   The statement is **False** from the information given.

2. Diesel cars generally emit smaller quantities of harmful gases than petrol cars.

   Cannot Say for certain from the information given whether the statement is true or false.

3. Cars without catalytic converters produce poisonous substances.

   The statement is **True** from the information given.

4. On balance, biofuels are more environmentally safe than ordinary fuels.

   The statement is **False** from the information given.

5. There is an abundant supply of hydrogen available.

   The statement is **True** from the information given.

Test 2 (Verbal reasoning)

1. False

   The text says "the reflector can be located and sometimes identified".

2. True

   The text says "Usually the higher the frequency, the sharper the return signal and the more accuracy can be obtained".

3. Cannot Say

   Although you may know that radar can be used in other areas, this is not stated in the text. From the passage in the box you cannot say whether radar has other uses.

Test 3 (Verbal meaning)

1. D (potato)

   Potato is a vegetable, the rest are fruit.

2. C (swim)

   All of the activities can be done on land except swimming, which is done in water.

Checking test 4

1. Name

   Overalls is misspelt in the copy list; the stock number is correct.

2. Correct

3. Number

   The stock number in the master List is 321957 but in the Copy List it is 312957.

Chapter 5. Numerical tests

Numerical test 1

1. What was the average number of visitors per month in the first three years after launch?

B) 6,121

2. How many of the site visitors spent three minutes or less browsing? (Note: give your answer as a number of visitors, not a percentage.)

D) 3.25

3. Based on the information given, what would you forecast the average number of pages visited to be in year 10?

D) 8,550

4. What percentage of visitors spent between four and 13 minutes browsing the site?

E) 38%

5. If the total number of visitors is 210,478, estimate how many browsed the site for less than 10 minutes. (Note: give your answer as a number of readers, not a percentage.)

C) 181,011

Numerical test 2

1. E (54)

6 x 9 = 54

2. D (24 litres)

4 x 2 x 3 = 24

Numerical test 3

1. 8 Miles

2. 4 Miles

Instead of travelling the 4 miles straight to port, it travels 5 miles South West and then 3 miles North. So the total distance travelled is 5 + 3 = 8 miles.

If the ship has travelled straight to port it would have travelled 4 miles. So the total additional distance travelled is 8 − 4 = 4 miles.

Chapter 6. Abstract reasoning and other tests

Abstract reasoning test 1

Answer: C

The triangles and the stars act as distracters; the quarter circle shape is the only one that moves in a sequence, from top of the box to the bottom. By doing so, the angle tips to the right by 45 degrees.

Abstract reasoning test 2

Answer: A

Group 1 has same colour shapes diagonally opposite each other but they are always four different symbols in a cell, like B and C in the answers provided.

Group 2 has the same colour symbols in each row and can have the same symbol in a cell. Like answer D.

Answer A fits neither criteria.

Abstract reasoning test 3

Answer: E

The logical sequences are:

Looking at the overall picture, allocation of arrows and diamonds follow a recurrent pattern. It helps to imagine what the column after the last one on the right would look like.

Looking at individual columns and rows:

In each column, from top to bottom, symbols change places to the opposite site of the following cell.

The ovals change colour from left to right from grey to white to grey. This helps to work out the colour of the oval in the missing cell. Ignore the colour of the arrows, there is no logical sequence.

There are no other logical relationships between symbols.